Corporate Governance

Risk Management by State-Owned Enterprises and their Ownership

This work is published under the responsibility of the Secretary-General of the OECD. The opinions expressed and arguments employed herein do not necessarily reflect the official views of OECD member countries.

This document and any map included herein are without prejudice to the status of or sovereignty over any territory, to the delimitation of international frontiers and boundaries and to the name of any territory, city or area.

Please cite this publication as:
OECD (2016), *Risk Management by State-Owned Enterprises and their Ownership*, Corporate Governance, OECD Publishing, Paris.
http://dx.doi.org/10.1787/9789264262249-en

ISBN 978-92-64-26221-8 (print)
ISBN 978-92-64-26224-9 (PDF)

Series: Corporate Governance
ISSN 2077-6527 (print)
ISSN 2077-6535 (online)

Photo credits: Cover © Vladitto/iStock/Thinkstock

Corrigenda to OECD publications may be found on line at: *www.oecd.org/about/publishing/corrigenda.htm.*

Foreword

Taking risks is a fundamental driving force in business and entrepreneurship. To reap the full rewards of risk-taking, however, firms need to have in place effective risk management practices. The effective implementation of corporate governance standards like the OECD Guidelines on Corporate Governance of State-Owned Enterprises (hereinafter "SOE Guidelines") should ensure that risks are understood, managed, and, when appropriate, communicated.

This report aims to identify practices employed by the SOE and by their government owners to prevent excessive risk-taking by SOEs in the broader context of their normal business operations. It reflects responses from 33 countries to a questionnaire on this subject, including: Argentina, Austria, Belgium, Brazil, Chile, Czech Republic, Denmark, Finland, France, Germany, Greece, Iceland, Ireland, Israel, Italy, Japan, Kazakhstan, Latvia, Lithuania, Mexico, Netherlands, New Zealand, Norway, Poland, Philippines, the People's Republic of China (hereinafter "China"), Portugal, Slovenia, Spain, Sweden, Switzerland, Turkey and the United Kingdom. The national contributions and the present report have been reviewed by the OECD Working Party on State Ownership and Privatisation Practices (Working Party), which developed and oversees the implementation of the OECD Guidelines on Corporate Governance of State-Owned Enterprises (the "Guidelines"). The information in the report is therefore based on self-reporting, but has been made subject to a peer review.

Information included in the report is current through July 2016, when the report was given final approval and declassified by the Working Party. It was prepared by Mary Crane-Charef with guidance from Hans Christiansen, both of the Corporate Affairs Division of the OECD Directorate for Financial and Enterprise Affairs.

Table of contents

Tables

Figures

Boxes

Acronyms, abbreviations and terminology

AGM	Annual general meeting
AGN	General Audit Office (Argentina)
APE	L'Agence des participations de l'État (France)
ASF	Auditoría Superior de la Federación (Mexico)
CEO	Chief executive officer
CFE	Comision Federal de Electricidad (Mexico)
CGPAR	Corporate Governance and Property Administration (Brazil)
CGU	Federal Control Unit (Brazil)
CNV	Comisión Nacional de Valores (Argentina)
COSO	Committee of Sponsoring Organizations of the Treadway Commission
DKK	Danish Krone
EUR	Euro
GCA	Government Companies Authority (Israel)
GOCC	Government-owned or -controlled corporations (Philippines)
ISO	International Organization for Standardization
JSC	Joint stock corporation
OECD	Organisation for Economic Co-operation and Development
OIC	Organisation for Internal Control (Mexico)
PEMEX	Petroleos Mexicanos
SAO	State Audit Office (Latvia)
SEP	Sistema de Empresas Públicas – Public Enterprises System (Chile)
SEST	Secretary of Coordination and Governance of State Enterprises (Brazil)
SIGEN	Sindicatura General de la Nación (Argentina)
SOE	State-owned enterprise
SSH	Slovenian Sovereign Holding

Terminology used in this report

This report focuses on a discussion of risk in the general sense. While recognizing that "risk", "risk management" and "risk governance" may have specific meaning for SOEs that are listed or operating in the financial sector, this report defines risk in the general sense as both financial risks (such as exchange rate risk) and non-financial risks, such as those identified in the Guidelines (i.e., public procurement risk [Guidelines III.G], compliance risk [Guidelines V.C], risk related to fulfilling responsible business conduct obligations [Guidelines V.D], conflict of interest risk [Guidelines V.E], risk associated with related party transactions [Guidelines VI.A.8]). Where possible, questionnaire responses and this report aimed to differentiate material differences in the treatment of risk given an SOE's legal status and/or sector of operations.

In addition, the definition of state-owned enterprises applied in this report derives from that provided by the SOE Guidelines, which define SOEs as "any corporate entity recognised by national law as an enterprise, and in which the state exercises ownership". This definition includes joint stock companies, limited liability companies, and partnerships limited by shares, as well as statutory corporations whose purpose and activities (or parts of their activities) are of a largely economic nature.

Finally, given that this report includes a specific assessment of the responsibility of SOE boards of directors in supervising SOE risk management, it may be useful to note that the term "board of directors" refers to the corporate body charged with the functions of governing the enterprise and monitoring management. Where relevant, a distinction is made between countries with a one-tier board system and a two-tier system. For the latter, the report aims to specify responsibilities relative to the board and those assigned to management (or "management board").

Executive summary

Taking risks is a fundamental driving force in business and entrepreneurship. To reap the full rewards of risk-taking, however, firms need to have in place effective risk management practices. According to a 2014 peer review of risk management corporate governance practices conducted by the OECD Corporate Governance Committee however, many firms continue to underestimate the cost of risk management failures. These costs may be greater in state-owned enterprises (SOEs), where the two main disciplining factors bearing on private firms – the risks of bankruptcy or hostile takeovers – are weaker or non-existent. In addition, public ownership may raise additional concerns about the degree of oversight, at the level of general government, over the actual and contingent liabilities vis-à-vis corporate risk management practices.

The effective implementation of corporate governance standards like the OECD Guidelines on Corporate Governance of State-Owned Enterprises (hereinafter "SOE Guidelines") should ensure that risks are understood, managed, and, when appropriate, communicated. The Guidelines emphasize the role of the Government, the board, management, shareholders and stakeholders in identifying and managing risk. The Guidelines are available online at: *www.oecd.org/daf/ca/soemarket.htm*. This report aims to identify practices employed by the state-owned enterprise (SOE) and by Governments that aim to prevent excessive risk-taking by SOEs in the broader context of their normal business operations. It builds on an earlier survey of SOE risk governance that was included in the Corporate Governance Committee's 2014 peer review of risk management corporate governance practices.

The Key findings section below provides a brief overview of key figures from the report's stocktaking of risk management practices employed by SOEs and their government owners. These results are largely consistent with the preliminary survey of SOE risk management practices reviewed by the Corporate Governance Committee in 2014. First, in Chapter 1, the report describes the legal and regulatory framework within which SOEs in the 33 participating countries operate. The stocktaking finds that, in general, the minimum legal and regulatory risk-management requirements for private companies also apply to SOEs, which are often subject to additional SOE-specific risk rules. In four jurisdictions, at least large SOEs are required to apply the same rules as listed, privately owned companies. Turkey reported that SOE-specific risk management rules were under consideration at the time of writing. Brazil edited four rules in 2016 addressing risk management to implement risk policy, audit committee and internal risk area in all SOEs.

Second, in Chapter 2, the report surveys risk governance at the level of the SOE, looking first at the responsibilities assigned to the board of directors to supervise management's establishment, implementation and monitoring of SOEs' risk-management processes. The report finds that, in just over half of reporting countries, boards are required to oversee the establishment of risk management systems (52%). A smaller percentage (42%) is required to establish a specialised board committee to oversee risk.

Practices for identifying and reporting risk to the board are fairly standard and generally reflect private sector practices.

Third, in Chapter 3, the report provides an overview of practices employed by the state to ensure effective risk governance in the SOE sector. Most reporting countries do not have an explicit risk tolerance level for their SOE portfolio, determining the state's risk tolerance level on an as-needed, case-by-case basis. This reflects many countries' tendency to rely on boards of directors or, in some cases, the annual general meeting (AGM) to define an SOE's risk appetite, which is also true regarding the setting of target rates of return and maximum leverage ratios for SOEs. Respondents also indicate that risk considerations do not generally factor into state practices for nominating and remunerating members to the board. Finally, ownership functions in responding countries were more active when ensuring the effective implementation of SOEs' internal risk management functions (either directly or indirectly), for example by reviewing risk management systems and subjecting them to state audit.

Key findings on risk management by SOEs and their ownership

- Legal & regulatory framework
  - 88% of the countries report that rules for risk management by SOEs are the same as, or similar to those applicable to private companies, while 58% apply or plan to apply additional risk-management rules to SOEs.
- Risk management at the level of the SOE
  - 52% of countries require SOEs to establish risk management systems (via laws, regulations, explicit policies or otherwise). 42% require large SOEs or certain categories of SOEs to establish a specialized board committee to oversee risk within the SOE (usually an audit and/or risk committee).
  - 18% require at least large SOEs to employ risk specialists (outside of or in addition to special rules for listed companies and/or financial institutions).
- Risk management at the level of the state
  - 15% of the responding countries formally set a risk tolerance level as regards the overall state ownership portfolio, for example Via a sector-wide and explicit law, regulation, or policy document or in the broader context of overall strategic planning. 82% describe practices for communicating risk tolerance levels vis-a-vis individual SOEs, the most common among these being deferring to the board of directors or AGM (38%) and/or communications between the SOE and the ownership function (26%).
  - Risk is explicitly factored into the setting of target rates of return and/or maximum leverage ratios in approximately one-third of countries.

- In 12% of countries, risk-management skills are only explicitly factored into director nominations and into director remuneration.

- 79% of the state owners reviewed their SOEs' internal risk management systems, most often via reviews carried out by the ownership function (32%) and/or SOE activity reports (29%).

- 67% report that state audit institutions conduct audits of SOEs and, in 77% of these countries, the audit may include a review of SOEs' risk systems. In less than a quarter of responding countries (24%), the ownership entity may also be audited for its supervision of SOE risk governance.

Chapter 1

Legal and regulatory framework applicable to risk governance of state-owned enterprises

This section provides an overview of the framework under which state-owned enterprises (SOEs) operate in the 33 countries contributing to this stocktaking report. As per the OECD Guidelines on Corporate Governance of State-Owned Enterprises, it also assesses the extent to which commercially oriented SOEs are expected to follow similar risk-management rules as private sector companies in similar situations.

Introduction

This section provides an overview of the framework under which SOEs operate in the 33 countries contributing to this stocktaking report. The contributors are OECD member countries and other regular participants in the Working Party on State Ownership and Privatisation Practices (see Foreword). This overview is important to the discussion of SOE risk management for two reasons: First, it contextualises the discussion of what rules and expectations apply to SOE boards and management when they address risk, beyond the SOE-specific framework imposed by the state ownership function. Second, it provides an albeit small insight into countries' application of the OECD *Guidelines on Corporate Governance of State-Owned Enterprises'* (SOE Guidelines) recommendation that SOEs operating on a commercial basis should be subject to the rules as comparable to private sector companies, in order to ensure a level playing field and fair competition in the marketplace. (See Table 1.1 at the end of Chapter 1 for a cross-country comparison of responding countries' legal and regulatory frameworks on risk.)

Survey of SOE risk management practices

In 28 reporting countries (85%), SOEs are generally subject to commercial law, largely because SOEs in most of the reporting countries (23) are similarly incorporated as private enterprises. In five reporting countries, SOEs are established via statutory legislation but are generally subject to company law, while in two countries statutory SOEs are subject to SOE-specific rules. (See Figure 1.1) These findings are somewhat consistent with the Working Party's 2014 survey of the size and sectorial distribution of SOEs in OECD and Partner Countries, which estimates that a little under half of SOEs (by value and employment) are majority-owned unlisted entities, roughly 31% (by value) of SOEs are majority-owned listed entities, while 21% are statutory and quasi-corporations.[1]

The majority of countries (29) report that risk rules for SOEs are generally comparable to those applicable to private companies. While only a very small percentage of majority-owned SOEs in these countries may be listed (an estimated 2%),[2] at least large SOEs in four jurisdictions (Chile, Netherlands, Norway, and Sweden) are required to apply the same risk rules as listed companies.[3] As noted in the 2014 Corporate Governance Committee review, this approach may reflect the fact that, while most SOEs may not meet the size threshold to apply the same rules as listed companies and/or are established to fulfil a specific purpose, governments expect at least large and strategic SOEs to apply specific risk rules.

Nineteen countries (59%) apply or plan to apply[4] SOE-specific risk rules. The largest number of these countries includes risk-specific guidance within the broader legal, regulatory and policy framework for SOE governance. For example, in Latvia[5] and Lithuania,[6] the *legal framework for SOE governance* includes risk-specific provisions. Similar instructions are included in *SOE-specific corporate governance codes* in Chile,[7] Ireland[8], and Slovenia[9]. Ireland's Code of Practice for Governance of State Bodies, for example, includes a chapter on "Risk Management, Accountability, Internal Control, Internal Audit". The application of the Code is adaptable according to an SOE's size, nature and scale of activities, and available resources, if agreed upon with the SOE's parent Government Department (i.e. the state ownership entity). In Iceland,[10] the Philippines,[11] and Poland,[12] similar guidance and/or risk management expectations are included in the *state ownership policy* (Iceland) and/or *state ownership guidelines or principles* (Philippines and Poland). In the Philippines, for example, the SOE risk management framework is guided by the Ownership and Operations Manual Governing the Government-owned or -controlled corporations (GOCC) Sector and the Code of Corporate Governance for GOCCs. Finally, in Switzerland, SOEs' state-decreed *strategic objectives* include as a standard objective an adequate risk management system. Here, 'adequate' is defined according to international risk-management standards, such as ISO 31000 or the equivalent.

Figure 1.1. **Legal forms of SOEs and applicability of commercial law**

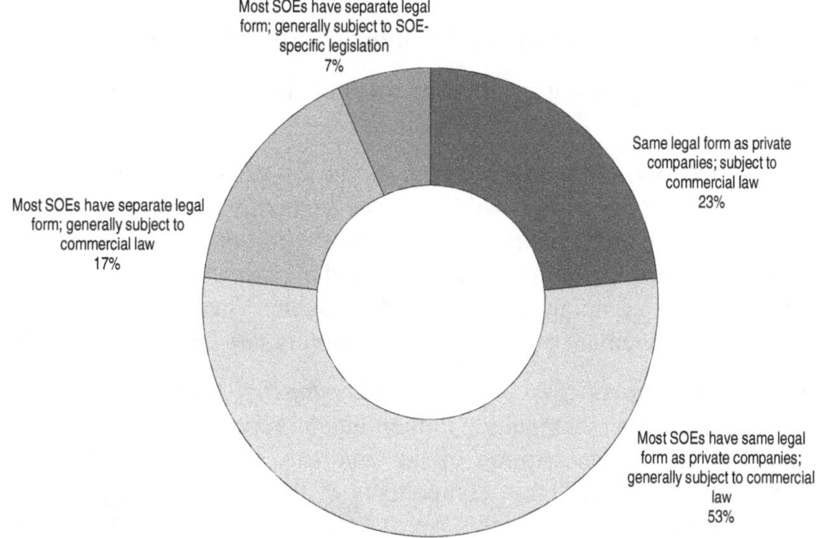

Source: Responses to the Working Party risk management questionnaire as of July 2016

In three countries (Argentina, Israel, and Mexico), SOE-specific risk rules are set forth in *standalone government resolutions or policy documents*. In Argentina, SOEs are subject to Resolution 37/2006, "Minimum Standards for Internal Control and Corporate Governance in State Enterprises and Companies", issued by the Comptroller General's Office (Sindicatura General de la Nacion).[13] In Israel, the 2009 Government Companies Authority (GCA) circular requires all Israeli SOEs – regardless of whether they are listed or the degree of their commercial orientation – to establish and regularly monitor a risk management process. Finally, in Mexico, the 2010 "General Guidelines for Internal Control" ("General Guidelines")[14] establish a standard model of internal control as a systematic process that must be implemented in each SOE. It applies to all SOEs without distinction, except "Productive State Enterprises", including Petroleos Mexicanos (PEMEX) and the Comision Federal de Electricidad (CFE).

Finally, in two countries (Austria and Germany), the SOE-specific risk rules are limited to *additional risk reporting* applicable only to SOEs. In Austria, for example, risk-management rules generally do not differ from those applicable to privately owned companies except that SOEs majority-controlled by the State are additionally required to submit quarterly reports with respect to their financial and non-financial key performance indicators. These reports include information on SOEs' risk management. Likewise in Germany, Section 53 of the Budgetary Principles Act (Haushaltsgrundsätzegesetz, HGrG) requires SOEs' certified accountants to report on risks as part of an "early warning system". These reports must be consistent with the German accounting standard IDW PS 720.[15]

Country case example: The risk framework for Swedish SOEs

In Sweden, where the state ownership portfolio comprises of 41 wholly owned and 8 partly owned companies, all SOEs are explicitly expected to apply the same risk-management standards as those for listed companies. This country case example: (i) describes the Swedish legal and regulatory framework applicable to SOE risk management; (ii) highlights the specific risk-management practices of certain Swedish SOEs; and (iii) describes how the State builds on SOEs' risk disclosures to monitor the SOE sector's exposure to risk and how this information is communicated to Parliament.

a. The Swedish legal and regulatory framework for SOE risk management

The following laws regulating risk management apply equally to listed companies and SOEs.[16]

Companies' Act (*Sw. Aktiebolagslagen*)[17]: The Swedish Companies' Act sets out that the board of directors is responsible for the company's organisation and for the management of the company's business. While not explicit on risk management, the Act also requires that the board continuously evaluate the company's financial position and that it ensures that the company is organised in such a manner that the company's bookkeeping, asset management and financial situation is satisfactorily controlled.

Act on Annual Reports (*Sw. Årsredovisningslagen*)[18]: According to the Act on Annual Reports, companies must include in their annual reports a management report that should outline *inter alia* a description of the company's *material risks* (which is not further defined), as well as the main components of the company's system for internal control and risk management. Under this Act, LLCs (and also applicable to SOEs) must also publish a company steering report describing the systems for internal control and risk management.

In addition to these laws, the Swedish State Ownership Policy[19] states that the Swedish Code on Corporate Governance should be applied in all SOEs in which the state has a controlling interest. (In SOEs where the state is a joint owner, the state ownership entity engages in dialogue with the other owner(s) to ensure that the State Ownership Policy is applied). Sweden is one of five jurisdictions participating in this stocktaking to report that at least large SOEs must apply the same risk rules as listed companies (along with Chile and Netherlands). In addition, the State's guidelines on external reporting for SOEs[20] holds SOE boards responsible for ensuring companies' accounting and reporting comply with the SOE external reporting guidelines, in addition to accounting legislation and generally accepted accounting principles. In addition, the external reporting guidelines require SOEs' boards to ensure that annual reports, interim reports and year-end reports are prepared in accordance with the rules of OMX Nordic Exchange Stockholm AB in the listing agreement. This means that the SOEs are required to present a corporate governance report and a statement on internal control in accordance with the Swedish Code for Corporate Governance.

According to the Code, it falls upon the board to ensure that there are efficient systems for monitoring and controlling the business of the company and any risks associated with the company's operations. Furthermore, the board is responsible for ensuring that the company has good internal control and formalized processes for financial reporting and internal control. In companies lacking internal auditors, the board must yearly evaluate the need to establish such a function. The motives must be made public in the company steering report.

Section 10 of the Code sets forth rules for the board's annual disclosure to shareholders and the capital market regarding corporate governance functions in the company and how the company applies the Swedish Corporate Governance Code. (The Code is enforced on a comply-or-explain basis.) This information is to be published in a corporate governance report and on the company's website. The corporate governance report must include a description of internal controls in accordance with paragraph 3 of rule 7.3 and with rule 7.4, which state:

> *7.3 (...) For companies that do not have a separate internal audit function, the board of directors is to evaluate the need for such a function annually and to explain its decision in its report on internal controls in the company's corporate governance report.*
>
> *7.4 The description of the company's internal controls included in the corporate governance report is also to include the board's measures for monitoring that the internal controls related to financial reports and reporting to the board function adequately.*

b. Examples of risk management reporting by three Swedish SOEs

(i) Vattenfall

Vattenfall is fully owned by the Swedish state and is one of Europe's largest generators of electricity. Vattenfall's main products are electricity, heat and gas. In electricity and heat, Vattenfall works in all parts of the value chain: generation, distribution and sales. In gas, Vattenfall is active in sales. The company also engages in energy trading.

Vattenfall includes in its annual and sustainability reports a specific report on risk and risk management within the company.[21] The company explains in its report that its enterprise risk management (ERM) system, which is based on the COSO standards, categorises Vattenfall's exposure to three main categories of risk and how these risks are mitigated (see also Figure 1.2):

- Strategic risk – such as a change in political control and changes in legislation and rules and regulations governing the energy industry.
- Operational risk – such as risks associated with operation and maintenance of electricity and heat production plants, high process safety, supplier cooperation, and competence succession and planning.
- Financial risk – such as currency risk, interest rate risk, electricity price risk, fuel price risk, and credit and liquidity risks.

Figure 1.2. **Vattenfall Risk Pyramid**

		Examples of risks	Examples of risk mitigation
Financial risk	Financial risk (short- to medium-term)	Electricity price risk Fuel price risk Volume risk Credit risk Liquidity risk Interest rate risk Currency risk Price risk in equities	Hedging of electricity and fuel prices Effective management of debt portfolio Analysis and selection of counterparties Risk mandate
Operational risk	Risks in operational assets and infrastructure, and personnel and organisational risks (short- to long-term)	Operational asset risk Security risk Personnel risk Legal risk Tax risk	Maintenance and renewals Optimisation of asset management Insurance High process safety Internal governance and control Succession and competence planning
Strategic risk	Risk for changes in political control, changes in public opinion, changes in rules and regulations, and risk in choice of technology (medium- to long-term)	Political risk Investment risk	Active business intelligence activities Diversified and sustainable production portfolio Scenario analyses in the strategic process

This illustration shows Vattenfall's general risk structure and indicates a relative net exposure/impact on the value of Vattenfall's production and distribution portfolio after suitable risk mitigation actions have been taken.

Source: Vattenfall Annual and sustainability report 2014. (See online here: https://corporate.vattenfall.com/globalassets/corporate/investors/annual_reports/2014/annual-and-sustainability-report-2014.pdf)

(ii) Swedish Export Credit Company (SEK)

SEK is a credit market institution that arranges financing for exporters and exporters' customers. The aim of all its business operations is to strengthen the Swedish export industry and Swedish competitiveness internationally by providing financial solutions to the Swedish export industry on commercial and sustainable terms. SEK offers loans to Swedish exporters, their subcontractors and foreign buyers of Swedish goods and services.

Figure 1.3. **SEK Risk Framework**

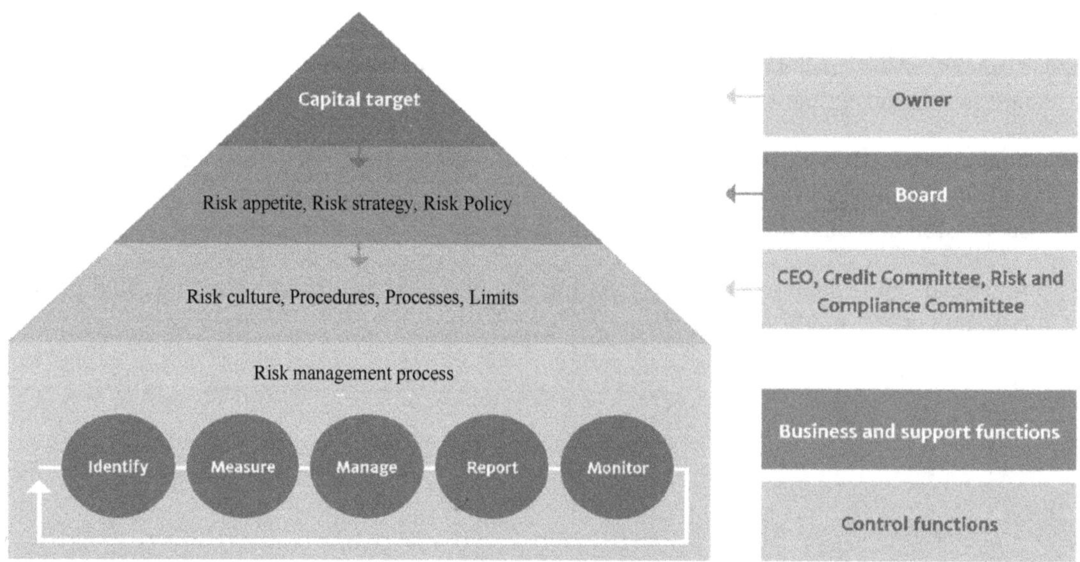

Source: SEK Capital Adequacy and Risk Management (Pillar 3) Report 2015 (See online here: http://www.sek.se/en/wp-content/uploads/sites/2/2016/02/SEK_Pillar3_2015.pdf)

SEK's annual reports[22] include an overview of the institution's core risk management principles, the risk framework and risk management process, along with a detailed risk statement. According to the company's risk report, SEK's board of directors "has ultimate responsibility" for the company's organization and administration, "including overseeing and monitoring risk exposure, risk management and compliance". The structure of SEK's risk framework (see Figure 1.3) is ultimately governed by SEK's mission from its owner, the Swedish state, and SEK's business model.

(iii) Telia Company

Telia Company is a global telecommunications services provider operating in Sweden, Europe and Eurasia. It is listed in Sweden and Finland and is 37.3% owned by the Swedish State.[23]

Telia Company's directors' report and corporate governance report, included in the company's Annual and Sustainability Report 2014,[24] defines risk as "anything that could have a material adverse effect on the achievement of Telia Company's goals. Risks can be threats, uncertainties or lost opportunities relating to Telia Company's current or future operations or activities." Telia Company's describes its ERM system as a three-line defence (integrated governance, risk management and compliance) that is "an integral part of the group's operational activities, business planning processes and monitoring of business performance". The aim of its ERM system, the company continues, "is not only to focus on risks from a negative perspective, but also to acknowledge that successful risk management is essential for strategy execution and sustainable growth." (See Figures 1.4 and 1.5)

Figure 1.4 Telia Company ERM "Lines of Defence"

Operational management practice
Internal controls
Revenue assurance
1st line
→
Risk management
Ethics and compliance
2nd line
→
Group internal audit
External audit
Regulatory supervision
3rd line

Source: Telia Company 2015 Annual + Sustainability Report (See online here: http://annualreports.Telia Company.com/en/2015/)

Figure 1.5. Telia Company ERM "Process Flow"

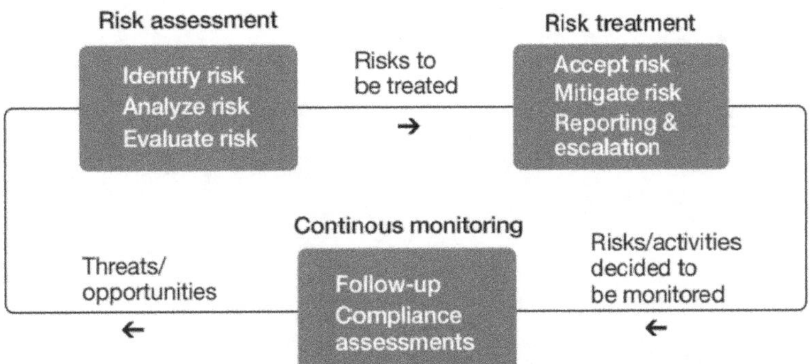

Source: Ibid.

The board and its audit committee play a key role in Telia Company's ERM system. These bodies review quarterly a consolidated risk report outlining Telia Company's major risk areas (categorised as financial, business-related, country-related and legal and regulatory risks). Each risk entry includes a risk description, mitigating activities, potential financial impact when possible, and a probability grading. At the level of management, quarterly Governance, Risk, Ethics and Compliance (GREC) meetings are organized at the group, regional and country level. GREC meetings are chaired by the CEO and they consist of Group Executive Management, including the head of the CEO office, the head of ERM, the Chief Ethics and Compliance Officer, as well as the Head of Internal Audit.

c. The State as a shareholder monitoring risk exposure in SOEs

SOEs' corporate governance disclosures under the Code are made on a comply-or-explain basis. These reports are not audited. The State shareholder monitors SOEs' compliance with the Code at least annually. The status of the entire State portfolio, including SOEs' ability to manage financial and non-financial risk, is included in the annual aggregate report on the SOE sector, which is submitted annually to Parliament.

The processes for monitoring and communicating the status of SOEs' exposure to risk, in particular, were under consideration by the Swedish Government in late 2015 / early 2016, following the conclusions in a June 2015 report[25] by Sweden's state audit institution, the Sw. Riksrevisionen, that the government should take a more active role in the governance of state-owned enterprises as regards risks and risk management. Its recommendations included improving communication to Parliament on risks and risk management in the SOE sector and providing an overall aggregate picture of risks in the SOE sector.

In response, Parliament received in December 2015 a proposal for addressing the state auditor's recommendations, including on improving communications to Parliament regarding SOEs' exposure to risk. The proposal includes improving the risk information contained in the aggregate annual report, including a description of external environment factors, but also industry-specific factors that may influence the SOE portfolio.

Table 1.1. **Legal and regulatory framework applicable to SOE risk governance (Q1-3; see Annex A)**

Country	Definition of risk (General v. material)	SOEs legal form (I,S)[1] / Application of commercial law (C)	At least large SOEs are required to apply the same risk rules as listed companies	SOE risk management is subject to specific risk rules[2]
Argentina	General	S / C		●
Austria	General	I / C		●
Belgium	General	I / C		
Brazil	General	S / C		●
Chile	General	I / C	●	●
China	General			●
Czech Rep.	General	I / C		
Denmark	General	I / C		
Finland	General	I / C		
France	General	I / C		
Germany	General	I / C		●
Greece		I / C		
Iceland	Material	I / C		●
Ireland	Material			●
Israel	General	I / C		●
Italy	General	I / C		
Japan	General	S / C		
Kazakhstan	Material			
Latvia	General	I / C		●
Lithuania	General	S		●
Mexico	General	S / C		●
Netherlands	General	I / C	●	
New Zealand	General	I / C		●
Norway	General	I / C	●	
Philippines	Material	S		●
Poland	General	I / C		●
Portugal	Material	S / C		●
Slovenia	General	I / C		●
Spain	General	I / C		
Sweden	General	I / C	●	
Switzerland	General	I / C		●
Turkey	General	I / C		(Forthcoming)
United Kingdom	General	I / C		

1. I = Most SOEs in the jurisdiction are incorporated; S = Most SOEs are statutory or quasi-corporations. C = SOEs are generally subject to company law.
2. SOE-specific risk rules may be codified in, for example, law, regulations, State decisions, or policy documents. These rules can be complementary to, or have precedence over, rules for risk management for private entities (where SOEs may be subject to both general commercial law and SOE-specific legislation).

Source: Responses to the Working Party risk management questionnaire as of July 2016; OECD (2014), and OECD (2012)

Notes

1. The data set for this publication does not include the following countries that participated in this stocktaking: Argentina, Brazil, Iceland, and Kazakhstan (OECD, 2014).

2. Figures relate to the total number of majority-owned listed entities as of 2012 in all participating countries except Argentina, Brazil, China, Iceland, Kazakhstan, and Philippines. OECD (2014) (Table 1.1).

3. A number of countries noted that SOEs are strongly recommended but not explicitly required to apply the corporate governance code for listed companies. In many of these cases, countries reported SOEs voluntarily apply these rules. In addition, many countries reported that SOEs operating in highly regulated sectors (such as finance) and listed SOEs must apply specific corporate governance rules.

4. Turkey reported that SOE-specific risk management rules were under consideration at the time of writing.

5. Under Latvia's 2014 Public Persons Capital Shares and Companies Law, SOEs must perform a risk analysis of their activities and include the results of this analysis in their three-year medium-term operations strategies.

6. SOE risk-management policies and practices are subject to the legal and regulatory SOE governance framework, including: the Law on State and Municipal Enterprises; Government Resolution No. 665, "On the Approval of the Procedure for the Implementation of Property and Non-property Rights of the State at State-owned Enterprises" (hereinafter "Ownership Guidelines");Government Resolution No. 1052, "On the Approval of the Guidelines for Ensuring Transparency of the Activities of State-owned Enterprises and Designating a Coordinating Authority" (hereinafter, "Transparency Guidelines"); and the Recommended Guidelines of the Financial Risk Management of State-owned Enterprises.

7. Under Art. 10 of Law No. 20.285 On Access to Public Information (2008), SOEs in Chile are required to disclose to the Chilean securities regulator, the Superintendencia de Valores y Seguros (SVS), the same information as that required of privately owned listed companies. In addition, the · Sistema de Empresas Públicas (SEP), which exercises the state enterprise ownership function in Chile, has developed Corporate Governance Guidelines for its SOEs. These Guidelines include guidance on issues including: the board and its chair; directors' duties; conflicts of interest; the audit committee; integrated risk management; fraud risks; prudential accounting policies; internal and external audit; and information security and people management.

8. All references to Ireland in this report refer to those SOEs that are designated bodies for the purposes of Part 3 of the National Treasury Management Agency (Amendment) Act 2014 and therefore within the remit of the New Economy and Recovery Authority (NewERA). These bodies include: Bord na Móna plc, Coillte Teoranta, Ervia (including Gas Networks Ireland and Irish Water), EirGrid Plc, and ESB. No input was provided in relation to the position of any SOE that is not within NewERA's remit.

9. The Slovenian Sovereign Holding (SHS), which manages the State's SOEs, adopted its Corporate Governance Code for Companies with State Capital Investment. It contains specific principles and recommendations relating to SOE risk management. For example, SOEs must have a risk register to assess risks and classify them

according to their importance, to determine responses to risks and responsible people for their implementation, to specify time limits for responses to risks, and to prepare risk reports.

10. Risk management by SOEs is addressed in the Government's 2012 general government ownership policy. Risk management codes are also outlined in the Government's 2009 policy for state-owned financial institutions, which requires the establishment of risk committees that report direct to the board of directors.

11. The GOCC Governance Act of 2011 provides the general policy framework for the risk management regime within the Philippine SOE sector.

12. Polish SOEs are expected to comply with the State Treasury's "Principles of Corporate Supervision over Companies with State Treasury Shareholding", which were adopted via Regulation No. 3 of the Minister of Treasury in January 2013 and which are addressed to SOEs' governing bodies. (2010 version available in English online here: *www.msp.gov.pl/en/corporate-supervision/2488,Principles-of-Corporate-Supervision-over-Companies-with-State-Treasury-Sharehold.html.)*

13. Available online here: www.sigen.gov.ar/documentacion/resoluciones_sigen/r37-06_anexo.pdf.

14. Available online here: *www.normateca.gob.mx/Archivos/66_D_3803_23-05-2014.pdf.* See also discussion of the Guidelines in box 1.4 of the Corporate Governance Committee's 2014 risk review.

15. IDW PS 720 requires reporting entities to answer · the following questions: "a) Has the business/group management defined early warning signs by type and scope and taken measures to use these signs for the timely detection of risks that pose a threat to the company's existence? b) Are these measures adequate and appropriate for fulfilling their purpose? Have indicators arisen showing that the measures are not being carried out?; c) Are these measures documented sufficiently?; d) Are the early warning signs and measures continuously and systematically calibrated and adapted to the current business environment and the company's processes and functions?"

16. Certain laws and regulations apply to SOEs operating in specific sectors, for example, financial and credit institutions. In the case of the latter, SOEs in Sweden (like SEK, below) are subject to the Banking and Finance Business Act (Lagen om bank- och finansieringsrörelse), which regulates among other things requirements regarding risk management and the responsibilities of the board to assure these requirements are fulfilled; EU Regulation No. 575/2013 of the European Parliament and of the Council of 26 June 2013 on prudential requirements for credit institutions and investment firms and amending EU Regulation No. 648/2012, which define requirements regarding capital adequacy and large exposures; and regulatory codes issued by the national financial services authority.

17. Available online (in Swedish) here: *https://www.riksdagen.se/sv/Dokument-Lagar/Lagar/Svenskforfattningssamling/Aktiebolagslag-2005551_sfs-2005-551/?bet=2005:551.*

18. Available online (in Swedish) here: *https://www.riksdagen.se/sv/Dokument-Lagar/Lagar/Svenskforfattningssamling/rsredovisningslag-19951554_sfs-1995-1554/?bet=1995:1554.*

19. See section 2.1 of the Swedish Ownership Policy, available on pages 122-125 of the Annual Report State-owned Companies 2014, available online here: http://www.government.se/reports/2015/12/annual-report-state-owned-companies 2014/.

20. See p. 126 of Sweden's *Annual Report State-owned Companies 2014.*

21. See, for example, the Vattenfall's risk management framework and pages 66-72 of the 2014 Annual and sustainability report, available online here: http://corporate.vattenfall.com/investors/risks-and-hedging/risk-management-framework/.

22. See, for example, pages 31-47 of SEK's 2014 annual report, available online here: www.sek.se/en/wp-content/uploads/sites/2/2014/01/SEK_%C3%85R_2014_en.pdf.

23. The Swedish State is the largest single shareholder in Telia Company, see online here for a breakdown of company shareholdings: www.teliasonera.com/en/investors/share/shareholdings/2016/1/shareholdings-as-of-december-31-2015/. Page 42 of Telia Company's 2014 Annual Report notes that, regarding the Swedish State's share ownership as a potential risk factor, "the Swedish State, acting alone, may have the power to influence any matters submitted for a vote of shareholders. The interest of the Swedish State in deciding these matters could be different from the interests of Telia Company's other shareholders."

24. See pages 41-46 for the presentation of risk in Telia Company's Annual and Sustainability Report 2015, available online here: www.teliacompany.com/en/investors/reports-and-presentations/annual-reports/.

25. Available online here: www.riksrevisionen.se/en/Start/publications/Reports/EFF/2015/-The-Governments-management-of-risk-in-state-owned-enterprises-/.

References

OECD (2014), The Size and Sectoral Distribution of SOEs in OECD and Partner Countries, OECD Publishing, Paris. http://dx.doi.org/10.1787/9789264215610-en org/10.1787/9789264208636-en.

OECD (2012), Competitive Neutrality: National Practices, www.oecd.org/daf/ca/50250966.pdf.

Chapter 2

Risk governance at the level of the state-owned enterprises

This section provides an overview of risk management rules and regulations applicable at the level of the state-owned enterprise (SOE), and how these rules are applied in practice. It includes, in particular, a focus on the role of SOE boards in overseeing how their SOEs identify and manage risk in their business operations, as well as practices for identifying and reporting risk to the board.

Introduction

The OECD Guidelines on Corporate Governance of State-Owned Enterprises (SOE Guidelines) posit that "severe difficulties" arise when state-owned enterprises (SOEs) undertake strategies without first clearly identifying, assessing, or reporting on related risks. "Without adequate reporting of material risk factors, SOEs may give a false representation of their financial situation and overall performance," the Guidelines further warn, which "may lead to inappropriate strategic decisions and unexpected financial losses."[1] SOEs' internal risk management systems should ensure SOEs' ability to identify, manage, control, and report on risks. These systems should also be equipped to apply to both financial and operational risks, "but also where relevant and material to the SOE, human rights, labour, environment and tax-related risks", as well as sector-specific risks.[2]

While SOEs' internal risk management systems may reflect their legal and regulatory environment (discussed in Part A) and the expectations of the state ownership function (discussed in Part C), they are ultimately implemented at the company level. A professional board of directors and capable management are necessary for identifying and mitigating unnecessary exposure to potentially harmful risk. This section therefore focuses, first, on the responsibilities of SOE boards of directors to supervise the establishment, implementation and monitoring of SOEs' risk-management processes. Second, it surveys practices in reporting countries for carrying out the SOE's risk-management processes. (At the end of Chapter 2, see Table 2.1 for a cross-country comparison of risk management responsibilities for SOE boards of directors in responding countries and Table 2.2 for a cross-country comparison of the SOEs' implementation of internal risk management systems.)

Overall board responsibilities

Expectations of SOE boards of directors in the 33 participating countries contributing to this report are in line with the Guidelines' recommendation that boards should be responsible for overseeing overall risk management, given their role as the enterprise's highest decision-making body. Specifically, the Guidelines state that, to carry out their role:

SOE boards should actively (i) formulate or approve, monitor and review corporate strategy, within the framework of the overall corporate objectives; (ii) establish appropriate performance indicators and identify key risks; (iii) develop and oversee effective risk management policies and procedures with respect to financial and operational risks, but also with respect to human rights, labour, environmental and tax-related issues; (iv) monitor disclosure and communication processes, ensuring that the financial statements fairly present the affairs of the SOE and reflect the risks incurred; (v) assess and monitor management performance; and (vi) decide on CEO remuneration and develop effective succession plans for key executives.[3]

This responsibility is codified to a varying degree across the 33 countries participating in this report, which represent a wide range of geographic regions and economies. Broadly, directors serving on boards and specialised committees in the 33 participating countries are expected to fulfil their duties – including risk oversight – vis-à-vis either the company (21 countries), the shareholder (1 country) or both (9 countries) (see Figure 2.1). These directors operate mostly in countries where private companies are expected to operate with one-tier board structure (16 countries), a two-tier structure (6 countries), the option to choose either (8 countries), or a hybrid structure (3 countries) (see Figure 2.2).

Figure 2.1. **Director "duty of care" in 33 countries**

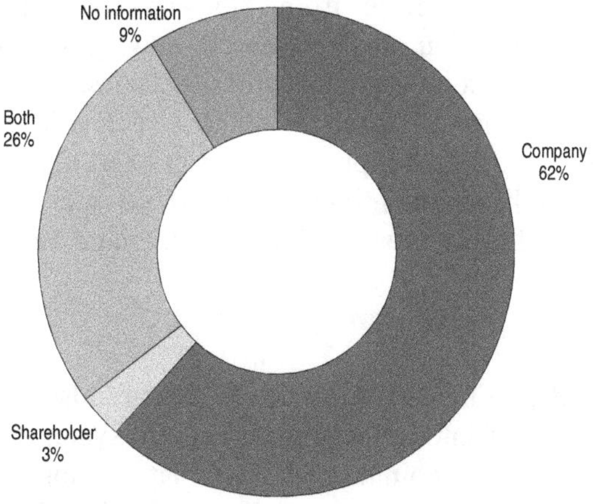

No information 9%
Both 26%
Company 62%
Shareholder 3%

Source: Responses to the Working Party risk management questionnaire as of July 2016

Figure 2.2. **Basic board structure for commercial enterprises in 33 countries**

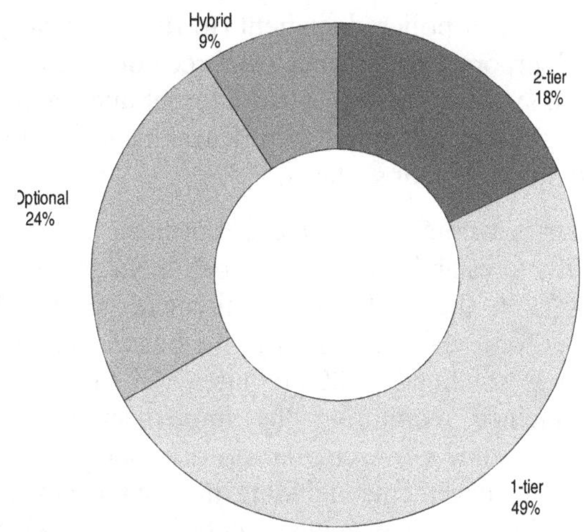

Source: OECD (2015a), and publicly accessible sources.

Requirement to establish specialised board committees

Responsibilities of SOE boards regarding risk oversight include the requirement in 14 reporting countries (42%) for at least large SOEs to establish a specialised board committee to oversee implementation of the SOE's risk management measures.[4] (In contrast, 62% of listed companies in OECD and Partner countries are required either by law, recommendation or listing rules to establish such committees (OECD, 2015b).[5]) In most of the reporting countries that have this requirement, SOEs meeting a certain size threshold or taking a certain legal form are most often required to assign risk oversight to an audit and/or risk committee.[6] In the Netherlands, for example, if the supervisory board consists of more than four members, it must appoint from among its members an audit committee, a remuneration committee and a selection and appointment committee, while in the Philippines all SOEs must establish a risk management committee as per the Code of Corporate Governance for GOCCs. In **Turkey**, un-listed private companies and SOEs must establish a specialised committee (audit or otherwise) if one is recommended by the independent external auditor.

In eight of the countries where SOEs are required establish a specialized board committee, these requirements derive from SOE-specific rules on risk that either complement – or are applied in lieu of – commercial law. (For example, these rules may be codified in SOE-specific resolutions or decrees, policies, SOE corporate governance codes, or SOE laws.) A number of countries without such a legal requirement reported that SOEs may be recommended to adopt such practices and that a number of large SOEs voluntarily establish specialised committees, even if no such requirements apply (for example, in Finland, Israel, Latvia, New Zealand, Switzerland, and the United Kingdom).

Requirement to establish internal risk management systems

Boards of directors of SOEs in 17 countries (52%) are also required to establish and oversee the implementation of internal risk management systems. In nine countries, this requirement is set forth either in commercial laws that are applicable to all enterprises, SOEs included, or in codes of corporate governance for listed companies, where these rules apply to SOEs (as in, for example, the Netherlands[7] and in Sweden[8]). But in a number of other jurisdictions, SOE-specific rules vest SOE boards with this particular responsibility. This kind of SOE-specific requirement appears most often in SOE-specific government resolution/decree or policy document (in five countries), and/or in SOE laws and regulations codes of corporate governance (in three countries)[9] (see Figure 2.3). In 16 reporting countries, these systems are subject to internal audit and/or to external audit.[10] (See Box 2.1 for one illustrative example[11] from Kazakhstan[12] of the role of the board in establishing internal risk management systems.)

In general, the countries with *SOE-specific government resolutions/decrees or policy documents* requiring SOEs to establish an internal risk management system can be broken down into two groups.[13] In the first, the requirement to establish an internal risk management system is set forth via instructions to the board (i.e., in Argentina and Israel). For example, Argentina's Resolution 37/2006 requires SOEs to establish audit committees, whose responsibilities include monitoring the implementation of an enterprise risk management policy. Israel's 2009 GCA circular on risk management assigns SOE boards the responsibility for risk management, including the establishment of risk management policies, approving rules for risk management reporting, reviewing the company's risk management system at least once yearly, commissioning comprehensive risk surveys, and overseeing updates to the risk management plan. In the second group, risk-management responsibilities are assigned directly to SOE managers (i.e., in Brazil and Turkey). In Brazil, recent rules published in 2016, Law 13.303/16 and Resolutions 12 and 18 of Brazil's SOE standard-setting body, the Inter-sectorial Commission for Corporate Governance and Property Administration (CGPAR),[14] require SOEs to have an independent audit committee and an internal area responsible for risk oversight and which reports directly to the board and management, respectively. In Turkey, the government's decree, the 2015 Annual General Investment and Financing Program, requires SOEs to establish an internal control system by the end of 2016. Finally, in Mexico, the General Guidelines provide instructions both at the level of the board and at the level of management: SOE boards of directors are responsible for examining documents related to risk management (i.e., the institutional risk management matrix, institutional risk map, work programs on risk management, and annual report of risk behaviour); updating the risk system; and if applicable, addressing comments by the Organisation for Internal Control (Órgano Interno de Control, OIC). SOEs must also establish as part of their management structure a Committee of Control and Institutional Performance, whose main duties relate to the implementation of the SOE's internal controls and risk management systems.

Box 2.1. **Kazakhstan: The role of Samruk-Kazyna's board in establishing a risk management procedures**

Kazakhstan's Sovereign Wealth Fund, Samruk-Kazyna, is a state-owned joint stock company founded in 2008 in order to manage the government's shares invested in state-owned national development institutions, national companies, and other legal entities, in order to maximize their long-term value and competitiveness in the world markets. Its board consists of eight members, including two independent directors, and is chaired by Kazakh Prime Minister Karim Massimov.[1]

According to Art. 8.10 and 8.20 of the Law of the Republic of Kazakhstan "On the National Welfare Fund", Samruk-Kazyna's board of directors approves the following documents on risk management for the enterprise:

- Samruk-Kazyna's risk management policy;
- Samruk-Kazyna's corporate system of risk management;
- Rules for identification of risk and risk assessment;
- Rules for currency exchange and interest rate risk management;
- Rules for managing credit risk on corporate counterparties;
- Rules for establishing country limits;
- Rules for establishing limits on balance and off-balance sheet liabilities for counterparty banks;
- Rules for the assessment and operational risk management for Samruk-Kazyna;
- Development of a register and mapping of critical risks and the Plan of Actions on their management for the projected year;
- Risk and control matrix for the projected year;
- Reports on risks (quarterly and at year-end).

Moreover, in accordance with the Law, the internal audit service is directly subordinate to the board of directors and reports on its work quarterly. The internal audit service implements the control, assessment and monitoring of risks on a permanent basis. When reporting on risk the internal audit service is also expected to formulate proposals to improve the effectiveness of risk management procedures. The reports on main risks include information on critical risks, plan of actions on critical risk management, and proposals for improving existing actions.

1. For the full list of Samruk-Kazyna's directors, see online here: http://sk.kz/fund_directors

Source : Kazakh authorities and Samruk-Kazyna's website.

SOE codes of corporate governance in Ireland and the Philippines also call on SOEs to which these codes apply to establish internal risk management systems. In Ireland, the Code of Practice for the Governance of State Bodies provides that SOEs should develop a risk management policy and that SOE boards should approve the risk management framework and should monitor its effectiveness. The Code enumerates some of the key elements of how this recommendation should be applied in practice, including how often the board should review the SOE's risk management; advice on board composition and organisation in order to address the SOE's risk position; and overseeing the establishment, implementation, and supervision of the SOE's approach to risk management, including the appointment of a Chief Risk Officer or a member of management with a direct reporting line to the board. Similarly, the Philippines'[15] GOCC Corporate Governance Code includes specific provisions on the board's responsibilities vis-a-vis risk management: Section 8 describes the functions of the board, including adopting and overseeing the implementation of risk management policies and programmes; Section 16 requires the establishment of a risk management committee, with responsibility for overseeing risk management functions and developing a risk management policy; and Section 43 requires GOCCs to maintain a website and post information on financial and operational matters, including material risk factors and measures taken to manage such risks.

A number of countries report that, even without an explicit requirement to establish an internal risk management system, a number of large SOEs have voluntarily implemented such measures. In the Czech Republic, for example, the risk management systems established by utility company ČEZ and energy distributor MERO address both financial and non-financial risks, including: "market risks (foreign exchange and interest rate risks, production/services of competitors in foreign countries, risk of changes in availability and prices of commodities); b) credit risks of financial partners and end customers; c) operating risks; d) entrepreneurial risks (strategic, regulatory and legislative risks, political risks of foreign countries where the company is operating or where it has its suppliers or customers, concentration risk); and e) reputational risk, etc." In Finland, many SOE boards voluntarily establish internal risk management systems and include risk management at least once per year on their agenda. In Latvia, a number of large SOEs have also voluntarily established risk management systems, which should support these enterprises' ability to implement Latvia's new SOE governance law requirement to include a risk analysis in SOEs' operations strategies.

Figure 2.3. **Sources of requirements for SOE boards to establish risk management systems**

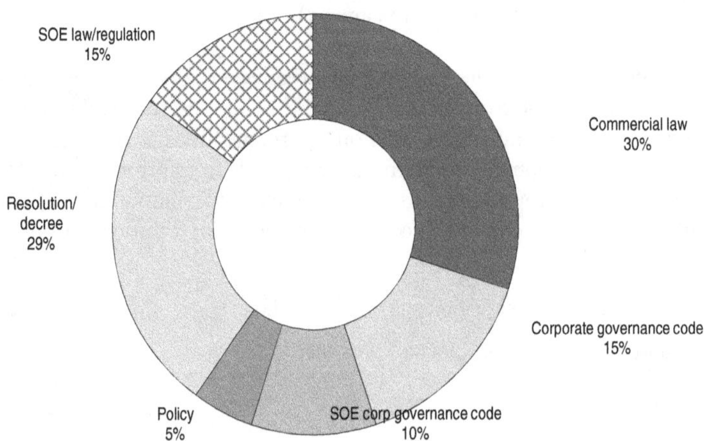

Source: Responses to the Working Party risk management questionnaire as of July 2016

Practices for identifying and reporting risk to the board

National practices for identifying and reporting risk to the board are fairly standard across the 33 countries and generally reflect private sector practices. Risk is most often identified by the audit or accounting function, by a specialised risk committee, or by management. These risks are usually reported to the board by management or a specialised committee. Risks are most commonly reviewed by the board on an annual, quarterly, and/or on an as-needed basis. (See Table 2.1 for highlights of risk-reporting practices in 11 countries.)

At the level of SOE management, six countries require at least large SOEs to employ specialised risk staff (i.e. a risk officer) (Brazil[16], Germany, Ireland, Israel, Kazakhstan,[17] and Philippines), though at least large SOEs in 15 reporting countries voluntarily establish a risk function within the enterprise (Belgium, Chile, China, Czech Republic, Denmark, Finland, Latvia, New Zealand, Norway, Poland, Spain, Sweden, Switzerland, Turkey, and the United Kingdom). This function can be voluntarily assigned to specialised risk staff (in seven countries); to senior management, for example the CEO or CFO (in five countries); and/or to specific business units (in three countries). (See Chapter 2.5 for examples of how SOEs in some of these countries have established risk management functions and procedures for how these functions report to the board.)

Table 2.1. **Highlights of risk-reporting practices employed by SOEs in 11 countries**

Country	Who identifies risks, and how?	Who reports to the board, how, and when?	SOE-specific risk requirements, if applicable
Austria		Under Austrian commercial law, applicable to SOEs and privately owned companies alike, the supervisory board receives its information mainly from regular and special reports from the management board, made on an annual, quarterly, and as-needed basis.	SOEs must file a quarterly report to their owner under the investment controlling regulation for majority participations of the Austrian state, which also includes information on their risk management, to which the supervisory board also has access. The reports include information on the risks to which the company is exposed, whether they may be avoided or not, a valuation of the risks, the probability of their occurrence, and a comparison with the recent period. Furthermore, the SOEs report whether the risk management is conducted in compliance with a certified risk management system.
Brazil	Risks are identified by a risk matrix for SOE audit planning that is prepared by Brazil's Federal Control Unit (CGU).	Risks are reported to the board by the audit Committee, in the frequency defined in the company's by-laws or board resolutions.	(See second column)
Chile	Companies identify their risks through a risk map that is developed by their internal audit units or the responsible unit for that function, which is subject to the knowledge and approval of the Board.	Risk factors are reported to the Board through the risk map and the periodic reports by the Audit Committee, the Internal Audit Unit, or the Compliance Officer, as the Board determines for each case. Each Board defines the frequency with which it should be informed by the Audit Committee, the	The SEP encourages its companies to have these reports at least quarterly, and that they should have an annual closure report. The SEP also encourages its companies to use in the preparation of the reports internationally recognized

Country	Who identifies risks, and how?	Who reports to the board, how, and when?	SOE-specific risk requirements, if applicable
		Internal Audit Unit or the compliance officer, and the type of report that will be required.	standards, such as standards set by the International Organization for Standardization (ISO) and by the Committee of Sponsoring Organizations of the Treadway Commission (COSO).
China	Most central SOEs have established regular risk assessment mechanism, and make risk assessments at least once a year. The assessment is conducted based on the company's strategy and objectives, as well as on an assessment of the macroeconomic and market environment. The risk management team will develop a consolidated risk assessment report and identify major risks after analysing the reports filed by various parties in this process.	The annual risk report is submitted to and reviewed by the executives meeting and finally approved by the board. Generally, preventing risk is one of the major tasks of the board. SOE boards have established rules and procedures, receive work reports, and the audit and risk management committees are deeply involved, so as to prevent, control and pre-assess major risks. Major operational risks are reported to the board by the risk management team on a regular basis.	SOEs' annual risk assessments are developed and conducted according to the Overall Risk Management Guidelines of Central SOEs, issued by the State-Owned Assets Supervision and Administration Commission (SASAC).
Czech Republic	Risks are mainly identified via expert risk assessments, in which the probability of the risk occurrence and the extent of adverse impacts on the company are assessed.	The results are reported (mostly in written form) to the board. Different risks are evaluated and reported with varying frequency: The most important risks are monitored daily, others weekly. Less relevant or more constant risks are evaluated on a monthly, quarterly or yearly basis.	
Denmark		The main channel for the board of directors to receive information on risk factors is through reports by management and auditors, which are typically made 5-10 times per year, depending on the company's size. In some companies, whistle-blower functions have been established as an alternative way to report certain categories of risks and incidents. The reporting can be both in form of quarterly financial reports, which are made public, and via internal reports prepared solely for the board.	
Kazakhstan[o]	The structural units of the Fund are responsible for identifying "key or critical risks".	The Management Board and Audit Committee agree, and the Board of Directors approves, a Risk Register that contains the Fund's key risks. This practice also adheres to the organizations of the Fund. The Fund submits quarterly risk reports to the Board of Directors.	"Key or critical risks" are defined by the Kazakhstan Sovereign Wealth Fund's Risk Management Policy.
Lithuania		SOEs managers are required to submit the enterprise's activity report for the reporting financial year, along with annual financial statements, to the board, if one exists, and the institution	The risk reporting requirements described here are set forth in the Law on State and Municipal Enterprises.

Country	Who identifies risks, and how?	Who reports to the board, how, and when?	SOE-specific risk requirements, if applicable
		exercising the ownership function. The activity report of an enterprise must include information about the main foreseeable risk factors and measures for minimising them.	
Slovenia	Management is required to identify risks and to set up a risk management system. The supervisory board's audit committee is usually assigned responsibility for monitoring the effectiveness of internal controls and the risk management system.	The Audit Committee reports to the Supervisory Board on its work and findings. If the Supervisory Board does not have an audit committee, then the effectiveness of the risk management system is monitored by the Supervisory board. The frequency of reporting by management on the system of risk management is not prescribed by law.	The Slovenian Sovereign Holding (SSH) Corporate Governance Code for Companies with State Capital Investment recommends that management report to the supervisory board on all significant risks and ways to manage them on a regular basis, and twice a year in non-public companies. The management should inform the Supervisory board about the risk management system at least once a year.
Switzerland	In general, the risk management process (specifically risk assessment) will not be conducted by the board itself but by specialized risk management functions, who report to senior management and the board.	The board of directors is ultimately responsible for the risk management of the organisation and has the competency to determine how material risk factors are identified, reported within the organisation, how often they are reported etc. The specifics for risk reporting therefore vary from organisation to organisation. The risk management process (described in column 2) might be complemented by a risk assessment of the top risks of the organisation, conducted by the board itself. The reporting frequency is determined by the number of board risk/audit committee meetings, generally at least twice per year	
United Kingdom	Risks are more likely to be identified by the Audit and Risk Assurance Committee. The Audit and Risk Assurance Committee needs to assure itself that it has effective communication with key stakeholders such as the Board, the Chief Internal Auditor, the Head of Internal Audit, any external auditor, the Risk manager and other relevant assurance providers	After each meeting of the Audit and Risk Assurance Committee, a report should be prepared for the Board summarizing the business taken by the Committee, explaining if necessary why that business was important, and offer the views of and advice from the Committee on issues which it considers the Board should be taking action. The reports should be copied to the Head of Internal Audit and any External Auditor. Reports are made quarterly, after each Audit and Risk Assurance Committee meeting.	

1. Responses from Kazakhstan reflect the views of Kazakhstan's Sovereign Wealth Fund, Samruk-Kazyna.

Source: Responses to the Working Party risk management questionnaire as of July 2016

Examples of SOEs' application of risk management policies and practices

The sections above described the rules and regulations incumbent on governments and SOEs' supervisory and management functions to establish, implement, and oversee the effectiveness of risk management systems within SOEs. This section aims to illustrate how, in some countries, SOEs have approached the question of how to implement these rules and regulations in practice. SOEs highlighted in this section are headquartered in the following jurisdictions: Belgium, Chile, France, Germany, Latvia, Poland, and the United Kingdom. As noted above in Chapter 2.3, most of the countries included in this section require SOE boards to establish a specialised board committee to oversee risk (Chile, France, Germany, and the United Kingdom), but only Germany requires the boards of its SOEs to oversee the establishment of internal risk management systems.

a) Belgium

BPost: Drawing up "lines of defence" for identifying and reporting risk

BPost, also known as the Belgian Post Group, is the Belgian SOE responsible for the delivery of national and international mail. BPost's internal control framework consists of a model with three lines of defence:

- First line: The design and maintenance of internal controls, which is under the responsibility of process owners;
- Second line: The internal control framework is then monitored by the company's Compliance, Internal Control and Risk Management function; and
- Third line: Internal audit provides a final review of the framework and reports independently and directly to the audit committee on a quarterly basis on audit results and on the status of follow-up of audit recommendations.

The legal basis for these reports can be found in Articles 96 and 526bis of the Belgian Companies Code.

b) Chile

Codelco: Identifying and mitigating copper price volatility risk

Codelco, an SOE fully owned by the Chilean Government, is the world's largest copper producer. The ability of Codelco and its government owner to mitigate harmful risk is integral to Chile's overall economy: Since Codelco was founded in 1971 until 2015, the company has produced 20% of all Chilean exports, it has delivered USD 116 billion to the Chilean State, and it serves as one of Chile's largest employers, with 18 000 employees and over 46 000 contractors' employees engaged in company operations.

One of the greatest risks facing Codelco (and, in relation, the Chilean economy) is the volatility of copper prices - a risk that both the company and the Government have tried to address via specific risk-management measures, described below. Copper price risks have a high impact in Codelco and their materialization affect decision-making and the company's results. Price fluctuations can have a significant effect on variables that include the company's strategic, tactical and operational emphasis, its mining plans and investment projects, sales revenues, costs, profits, contribution to fiscal revenues and investment and financing needs.

Copper prices have historically been subject to wide fluctuations. The price is affected by numerous factors beyond Codelco's control, including international economic and political conditions, supply and demand levels, the availability and costs of substitutes, inventory levels maintained by producers and others, and other actions by commodities markets participants. To a lesser extent, the copper price is also affected by the carrying costs of inventories and currency exchange rate movements.

In consultation with the State, the company takes a number of measures to address copper price volatility risk, including:

- Cost control and constant efforts to increase productivity in order to position its operations and projects in the lower part of the industry cost curve.
- Contracts designed with large components of variable costs (operational leverage).
- Avoidance of excessive borrowing (financial leverage) and the related financial burden (fixed cost.)
- Constant improvement of short and medium-term forecasts, and regular updating of planning parameters (Commercial Guidelines).
- Flexibility in the design and implementation of large investment projects.
- Robust and flexible mine planning through the incorporation of price risk in the preparation of plans.

c) France

Electricité de France (EDF): Creating a specific division to manage and control risk

While French SOE boards of directors are not required to establish and oversee risk management systems, some large SOEs voluntarily apply such measures, including EDF. In 2003, EDF established an overarching process for managing and controlling its operating (e.g. industrial, environmental and health), financial and organisational risks, with the aim of improving existing procedures, in particular by creating the Corporate Risk Management Division (DCRG). The DCRG is primarily responsible for:

- Ensuring that each Group entity carries out risk mapping, either directly for the EDF scope and that of the controlled subsidiaries, or through the governance bodies for the regulated subsidiaries and jointly-controlled affiliates, and establishing and updating the consolidated risk mapping of the Group's major risks;
- Warning the Chairman and Chief Executive Officer and the Executive Committee of emerging risks and risks that have not been adequately identified;
- Consolidating the deployment of the risk control policy, either directly within the EDF scope and that of the controlled subsidiaries, or through the governance bodies for the regulated subsidiaries and jointly-controlled affiliates in particular by ensuring the comprehensiveness and consistency of the various sectorial risk control policies;

- Ensuring the deployment of the internal control policy and steering the internal control function;
- Ensuring the deployment of the energy market risk policy within the EDF scope and that of the controlled subsidiaries and, more generally, ensuring the control of these energy market risks either directly within the EDF scope and that of the controlled subsidiaries, or through the governance bodies for the regulated subsidiaries and jointly-controlled affiliates;
- Defining and implementing financial risk control (interest, currency exchange, liquidity, equities and credit risks) and counterparty default risk control for the EDF scope and that of the controlled subsidiaries and ensuring the control of these financial risks through the governance bodies, for the regulated subsidiaries and jointly-controlled affiliate;
- Managing the comprehensiveness and relevance of the risk analyses performed on long-term investment and commitment projects, which are submitted to Executive Committee-level bodies for approval;
- Ensuring the deployment of the crisis management policy for the EDF scope and that of the controlled subsidiaries, and defining the terms of exchange and coordination with all subsidiaries during periods of crisis and guaranteeing the operational readiness of the crisis management system at Group level; and
- Defining, coordinating and deploying the prevention and control systems that are needed to manage risks of fraud and commercial non-compliance (corruption, money laundering, financing of terrorism, compliance with international sanctions, etc.); ensuring the management of these risks for the perimeter of EDF and its controlled subsidiaries, as well as for planned investments and commitments, in conjunction with the Legal Division.

d) Germany

Deutsche Bahn: Assessing, reporting, and publicly disclosing exposure to risk

The principles of Deutsche Bahn's (DB) risk management are laid down by corporate management and implemented throughout the DB Group. Additionally, there is a risk report and a management assessment of the risk situation. The assessment of the current risk situation is based on the risk management system.[18] An assessment of Deutsche Bahn's risk situation is publicly available on the company's website. (See Figure 2.4)

Figure 2.4. **Deutsche Bahn's risk situation assessment as of 31 December 2015**

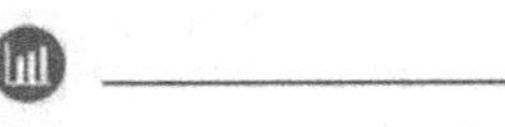

Opportunity and risk portfolio 2016 financial year as of Dec 31, 2015 [€ billion]

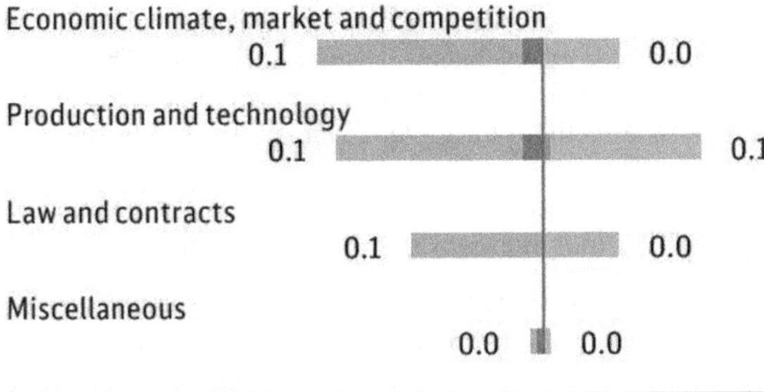

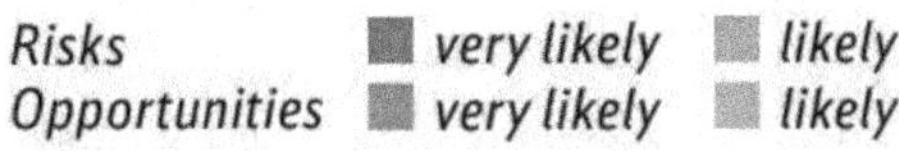

Risk portfolio 2015 financial year as of Dec 31, 2014 [€ billion]

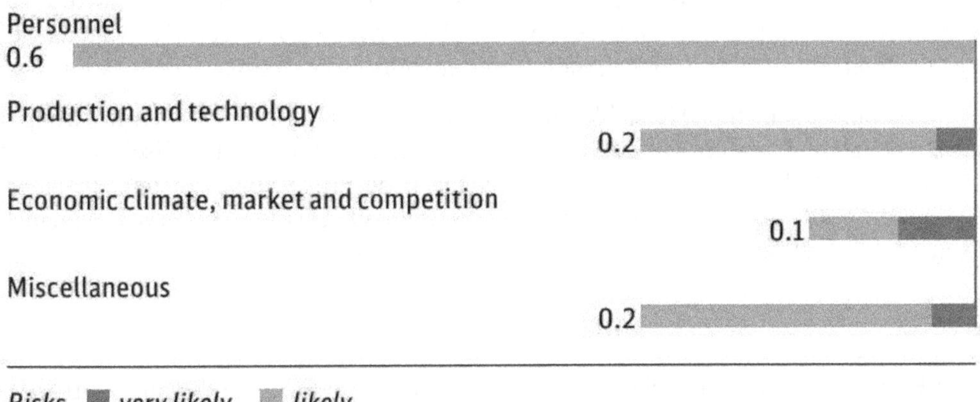

Risks very likely likely

Source: Deutsche Bahn 2015 Integrated Report (See online here: http://ib2015.deutschebahn.com/ib2015-en/group-management-report/opportunity-and-risk-report/major-opportunities-and-risks.html)

e) Latvia

Latvia State Forests (LVM): Assigning risk responsibilities throughout the SOE

LVM is one of Latvia's largest SOEs. It is responsible for the administration of state-owned forest property and the management of public forests and is fully owned by the Latvian Ministry of Agriculture.

LVM has voluntarily established a system for assigning responsibility for risk management throughout the company and for establishing procedures for reporting risk. The corporate planning department is responsible for planning and controlling, which requires carrying out SWOT ("strengths, weaknesses, opportunities and threats") analysis and analysing and preparing market forecasts. This unit reports directly to the vice president. LVM's internal audit operates as an independent unit, regularly reporting to the management board on the results of risk management and internal audits. The security division includes an information system security officer, who undertakes risk identification and control and reports directly to the CEO. Occupational safety specialists also report to top-level management.

Latvenergo: Applying the group risk management system in practice

Latvenergo's Group Risk Management Policy calls for the establishment of a risk management system. The risk management system provides that each organizational unit/department identifies and assesses risks within their activity scope and reports to a risk manager on those risks that are identified as "material". All material risks and their assessments are consolidated by the Risk Manager and presented to the Risk Management Committee. This committee sits at the executive management board level and is comprised of executive directors, who are also members of the executive management board; the director of internal audit and compliance; the corporate strategy director; and the risk manager. Top-priority risks are analysed in further detail and are reassessed by working groups set up from professionals/experts from different Latvenergo Group organizational units/ departments. The results of the more detailed risk analysis, as well as proposals for a plan for material risk mitigation activities are presented to the Risk Management Committee for their review, to the Latvenergo Executive Management Board for final approval, and to the Audit Committee for information.

The risk management system, like all other systems within the Latvenergo Group, is audited by internal audit. All Latvenergo Group material risks are disclosed to the company's stakeholders and general public in the Base Prospectuses of bonds issuance programmes published on Latvenergo and NASDAQ OMX Riga stock exchange websites.

f) Poland

Grupa Polski Holding Nieruchomości: Elements of one SOE's internal control system

Grupa Polski Holding Nieruchomości S.A., a listed real estate SOE incorporated as a joint stock company), has a developed system for key risk management to address operational, legal and financial risks. Elements of the risk management system include, *inter alia*, decision-making limits and the requirement of legal assessment and financial and accounting assessment of all significant operations. The process of monitoring the performance of internal control systems, internal audit and risk management is monitored by the supervisory board through the audit committee. Within the framework of fulfilling its supervisory function, the audit committee cooperates with the certified auditor. Within the framework of monitoring the internal control system, in the organisational structure of the company, Grupa Polski Holding Nieruchomości S.A has established an independent internal audit function, which reports directly to the supervisory board.

g) United Kingdom

Nuclear Decommissioning Authority (NDA): Identifying and mitigating risk in the nuclear sector

The NDA has an extensive internal risk management system covering operational plant failure (with subsequent impacts on commercial income); nuclear accident or incident, security and safety breaches and oversight of complex construction projects. NDA's assurance of the projects and programmes of its subsidiaries and sites is reviewed by its internal challenge function (reporting to its Board via the relevant Director). External audit / review is undertaken in two main ways: through the National Audit Office (and subsequently the Public Accounts Committee) or via the Infrastructure & Major Projects Authority for specific projects. A recent example would be NDA's approach to approving a new commercial model for its largest site, Sellafield.

URENCO: Working with the board and management to establish and monitor risk controls

The senior management and the Board of URENCO, a uranium fuel processor, have developed a detailed Governance, Risk and Control Framework. A Group Business Assurance function has been established, which is responsible for risk management and business continuity. Its Risk Management Committee reviews the Group's top risks, their controls and planned actions, and reports back to the Audit Committee and Board on a regular basis. These systems are reviewed by the SOE's external auditors, who provide reports to the Audit Committee. These reports are used by the SOE to assess the adequacy and effectiveness of its internal controls. An example is foreign exchange translation risk. The Group Business Assurance Function, alongside Group Treasury, reviews the SOE's exposure regularly and has developed and amended a hedging strategy, which the external auditors review and provide comment against.

Green Investment Bank (GIB): Voluntary financial risk controls in the finance sector

As a financial institution that invests for a commercial return, GIB takes risk very seriously and has a number of measures in place to ensure they are sufficiently monitored. Whilst GIB plc is not regulated, it adopts financial regulation best practice. GIB has a Chief Risk Officer responsible for monitoring risks, and there are a suite of risk measurement tools that monitors each of GIBs c60 investments, in addition to internal and operational matters. Such risks are reported to the Board, and for risk reports for investments reported to the Investment Committee. They also have an internal audit team that examines different areas of the business on a project by project basis, the results of which are reported to the CFO and Board.

Table 2.2. **Risk management responsibilities assigned to SOE boards of directors (Q4-7; see Annex A)**

Country	Duty of loyalty (C/S/B)[1]	Board required to establish specialized committee to oversee risk[2]	Board required to establish and oversee risk management system[2]	Rules for Identification and reporting of risk to boards of directors		
				Risks identified by:	*Risks are reported to the board by:*	*Reports to the board are made:*
Argentina	B	○	●	– Risk committee	– Risk committee – Sr. management	– Annually – As needed
Austria	C			– Management	– Management	– Annually – Quarterly – Ad hoc/as needed
Belgium	C	○				
Brazil	B	○	●	– Audit committee – Audit/accounting – Risk committee	– Audit committee –	
Chile	B	○		– Audit/accounting	– Internal audit – Risk / compliance function – Audit committee	– Quarterly – Annually
China	C			– Management – Risk committee	– Management	– Annually – Ad hoc/as needed
Czech Rep.	C					– Quarterly – Annually – As needed
Denmark	B	○	●	– Management – Audit/accounting – Whistle-blowers	– Audit – Management	– Monthly – Quarterly
Finland	C			– Management – Risk committee	– Management – Risk committee	– Annually
France	C	○		– Risk committee – Audit/accounting		
Germany	B	○	●	– Audit/accounting	– Audit	– Annually
Greece						
Iceland	B					
Ireland	C		●			
Israel	C		●	– Risk function – Risk committee – Audit/accounting	– Risk function – Risk committee – Audit/accounting	– Annually
Italy						
Japan	C					
Kazakhstan	B	○[3]	●[3]	– Management – Audit/accounting	– Management – Audit/accounting	– Quarterly – Annually

Country	Duty of loyalty (C/S/B)[1]	Board required to establish specialized committee to oversee risk[2]	Board required to establish and oversee risk management system[2]	Rules for Identification and reporting of risk to boards of directors		
				Risks identified by:	*Risks are reported to the board by:*	*Reports to the board are made:*
				– Risk function		
Latvia	S					– Annually
Lithuania	C / B[4]	O		– Audit/accounting	– Management	– Annually
Mexico		O[5]	●		– Sr. management	– Annually
Netherlands	C	O	●	– Audit/accounting	– Management	
New Zealand	C					
Norway	C		●	1 Management 2 Audit/accounting 3 Whistle blowers	4 Management 5 Audit/accounting	6 Annually 7 As needed
Philippines	C	O	●	– Risk function	– Risk function	– Annually – As needed
Poland	C			8 Management 9 Audit/accounting	10 Management 11 Audit/accounting	– Annually – As needed
Portugal	C					
Slovenia	C		●	– Management	– Management – Audit committee	– Semi-annually – Annually – As needed
Spain	C	O		– Management – Audit/accounting	– Management – Audit/accounting	
Sweden	C		●	– Audit/accounting	– Management	– As needed
Switzerland	B		●		– Compliance / risk function	– Semi-annually
Turkey	C	O[6]	●	– Management – Risk committee	– Management – Risk committee	– Every 2 months – As needed
United Kingdom	C	O		– Audit/accounting – Risk committee	– Risk committee	– Quarterly

1. C = company, S = shareholder, B = both
2. Entries in these columns are made when at least all large SOEs are required to establish specialized committees and internal risk management systems.
3. Requirements for the board to establish specialised risk committees and to establish and oversee risk management systems apply only to joint stock corporations with state participation.
4. Directors of SOEs established as LLCs must act in the interest of the company and its shareholders; directors of state enterprises must act in the interest of the company.
5. This requirement applies to Mexico's development banks (under Art. 70 of the United Banking Regulations), in addition to Petróleos Mexicanos (PEMEX) and Comisión Federal de Electricidad (CFE).
6. Turkish SOEs are required to establish a risk committee if recommended by the enterprise's independent external auditor. This requirement is applicable as of 2015 with the government's Decree on the 2015 Annual General Investment and Financing Program.

Source: Responses to the Working Party risk management questionnaire as of July 2016.

Table 2.3. **Implementation of internal risk management systems (RMS) (Q8-9; see Annex A)**

Country	Requirement to employ specialised risk staff (i.e., risk officer)	In countries where there is no requirement, the risk function is voluntarily established and assigned to:			RMS subject to:	
		Specialised risk staff	*Senior (C-level) management*	*Business units assigned specific risks*	*External audit*	*Internal audit*
Argentina						
Austria						
Belgium		○	○			
Brazil	●	○			●	
Chile		○			●	●
China		○				
Czech Rep.		○			●[1]	
Denmark		○				
Finland			○		●	
France						
Germany	●					
Greece						
Iceland						
Ireland	●					
Israel	●				●	●
Italy						
Japan						●
Kazakhstan	●[2]				●[2]	●
Latvia				○		
Lithuania					●	
Mexico						●
New Zealand						
Netherlands						
Norway		○				
Philippines	●					●
Poland		○			●	●
Portugal					●	
Slovenia						
Spain				○		
Sweden		○			●	
Switzerland			○		●	
Turkey			○		●	●
United Kingdom			○[3]			●

1. This mostly applies to SOEs operating in the finance sector.

2. Audits may be undertaken pursuant to the Law on State Audit and Financial Control (November 2015). Under this law, the State may conduct audits of state enterprises, LLPs and JSCs with State participation. As implementation of this new law progresses, it will be seen whether it may apply to quasi-State entities, Kazakh authorities reported as of July 2016.

3. In public corporations, it is typically the Chief Executive who has the responsibility to develop and implement effective risk management for the SOE.

Source: Responses to the Working Party risk management questionnaire as of July 2016

Notes

1. See the annotations to Chapter VI.A.6 of the SOE Guidelines.
2. Annotations to Chapter VI.A.6 also note that SOEs in extractive industries should disclose their reserves according to best practices in this regard, as this may be a key element of their value and risk profile.
3. See Chapter VII.B of the SOE Guidelines and annotations.
4. In one reporting country, Kazakhstan, this requirement only applies to joint stock corporations (JSCs) with state participation. JSCs are just one of four legal forms that SOEs can take in that jurisdiction.
5. See page 83 in *OECD Corporate Governance Factbook 2015* (OECD 2015), www.oecd.org/daf/ca/Corporate-Governance-Factbook.pdf.
6. These requirements refer to those applicable to SOEs regardless of whether they are listed or whether they operate in the financial sector. In nearly all responding jurisdictions, all listed entities and all financial sector entities – private sector or government-owned – were required to establish some kind of body at the level of the board for risk oversight.
7. The Dutch Code of Corporate Governance, which SOEs are required to apply, calls on companies to establish an internal risk management and control system "that is suitable for the company". This system should include: "a) risk analyses of the operational and financial objectives of the company; b) a code of conduct which should be published on the company's website; c) guides for the layout of the financial reports and the procedures to be followed in drawing up the reports; and d) a system of monitoring and reporting." The scope of the risk management system is not specified, as these guidelines apply for a broad range of companies of various sizes and activities.
8. Swedish SOEs are, like privately owned companies, subject to the risk management framework provided by the Swedish Companies Act, the Swedish Act on Annual Reports, and the Corporate Governance Code.
9. As noted previously, additional risk-management requirements often apply to listed SOEs and SOEs operating in highly regulated or higher-risk sectors like the finance industry.
10. As noted above, the degree of these requirements (i.e., obligations versus recommendations) varies in many countries from sector to sector, and according to whether SOEs are listed. Countries included here are those that apply these requirements to SOEs regardless of or in addition to – requirements on SOEs that are listed or operating in sectors like the financial sector.
11. For note, country or SOE examples in this report are included to illustrate how certain practices are applied in practice. Their inclusion does not represent a qualitative assessment (positive or negative) of these practices.
12. Kazakhstan's responses to this stocktaking were submitted by the Ministry of National Economy and supplemented by responses also submitted by Samruk-Kazyna, the Kazakh National Wealth Fund.
13. The risk-specific resolutions, decrees and policy documents referenced here are described more fully in Chapter 1 above.

14. Available online here: *http://antigo.planejamento.gov.br/ministerio.asp?index=4&ler=t3970*

15. The GOCC Corporate Governance Code elaborates on the higher-level recommendation in the 2011 GOCC Governance Law that requires GOCC Governing Boards to establish, oversee and render reports on their internal risk management systems.

16. Brazil edited four rules in 2016 addressing risk management to implement risk policy, audit committee and internal risk area in all SOEs.

17. The Kazakh authorities report that this requirement only applies to JSCs with state participation. Further, SOEs within the portfolio of the Kazakh National Wealth Fund, Samruk-Kazyna, are required to have specialized risk staff as per the Fund's own risk management policy.

18. See more online here: *http://ib2014.deutschebahn.com/ib2014-en/group-management-report/opportunity-and-risk-report/major-opportunities-and-risks.html.*

References

OECD (2015a), OECD Corporate Governance Factbook 2015, *www.oecd.org/daf/ca/Corporate-Governance-Factbook.pdf.*

OECD (2015b), OECD Guidelines on Corporate Governance of State-Owned Enterprises, 2015 Edition, OECD Publishing, Paris. DOI: *http://dx.doi.org/10.1787/9789264244160-en.*

Chapter 3

Risk governance at the level of the state

This section provides an overview of risk management practices employed by state-owned enterprises' (SOEs) government owners. This includes discussion of the state's determination and communication of its risk tolerance levels, the extent to which the state as shareholder reviews SOEs' risk management systems, and finally, the role of state audit institutions in the oversight of risk management in the SOE sector.

Introduction

Chapter II.F.3 of the OECD Guidelines on Corporate Governance of State-Owned Enterprises (SOE Guidelines) recommend that "[The state's] prime responsibilities [as an informed and active owner] include: setting and monitoring the implementation of broad mandates and objectives for SOEs, including financial targets, capital structure objectives and risk tolerance levels."

This section provides explores how certain countries apply this recommendation in practice, particularly as regards to ensuring effective risk governance in the SOE sector. It does so by looking at how governments: (1) determine and communicate their risk tolerance level vis-à-vis specific SOEs and/or the entire SOE sector, including through the setting of SOE target rates of return and leverage ratios; and (2) ensure effective risk governance at the level of the SOE, including via the ownership function's review of SOEs risk management systems and board nomination and remuneration policies, and by subjecting SOE risk practices to review by state audit institutions.

Determining and communicating the state's risk tolerance level

Most countries do not have a sector-wide, explicit risk tolerance level for their overall ownership stake in the SOE sector: Five reporting countries set their overall risk tolerance level either in the context of overall strategic planning (Chile, China, and Lithuania) or via a sector-wide law, regulation or policy (Philippines and Poland). For example, in the Philippines, the parameters for the State's risk tolerance level are provided for in the GOCC Governance Act, while in Poland, the state's risk tolerance level is determined in government resolutions concerning management control at the Ministry of Treasury. Under the resolution, SOE-related risks are identified in the Ministry's "risk register" and published on the Ministry's internal website. (At this end of this section, see Table 3.1 for a cross-country comparison of practices for determining and communicating the state's risk tolerance level and Table 3.2 for a cross-country comparison of whether and how governments consider risk tolerance levels when setting rates of return and leverage ratios.)

Governments communicate their risk tolerance level as regards the state's ownership stake in individual SOEs in a variety of ways. Governments may use more than one channel of communication with their SOEs. These can include: deferring to, or participating in decisions made by the board or AGM (16 countries); direct communications between the ownership function and the SOE (11 countries); providing risk-taking guidelines (4 countries); via the extent of state guarantees (3 countries); and/or state control over major transactions (3 countries) (see Figure 3.1).[1] For example, in Denmark, the Government established a specific level of risk exposure toward one SOE's activities in foreign markets. The risk tolerance level was defined such that, among other conditions, no single contract could exceed 0.5 billion DKK[2] (EUR 67 million) and the total amount of contracts could not exceed more than 15% of the company's equity. In Switzerland, the state's risk tolerance level for individual SOEs may be expressed in the SOE's legal mandate and in the SOE's strategic objectives, which specify risk-related factors, such as the scope of the SOE's activities or the net debt ratio. Finally, in Chile, the Government recognises that Codelco's (see Chap. 2.5.b) exposure to copper price volatility is high and, given this SOE's role in the Chilean economy, the Chilean economy is therefore highly exposed to fluctuations in copper prices. To mitigate harmful effects of this risk, the Government sets Codelco's threshold vis-à-vis copper price volatility via fiscal policy.[3]

Target SOE rates of return and leverage limits may also serve as indicators of the state's risk tolerance level and expected risk/reward ratio for a particular SOE. Ten countries report that they consider the state's risk tolerance level when setting SOEs' target rates of return (Chile, China, Denmark, Ireland, Latvia, Lithuania, Netherlands, Norway, Philippines and Slovenia), and eight countries apply similar considerations when setting SOE leverage ratios (Chile, China, Ireland, Lithuania, Netherlands, Philippines, Slovenia, and Switzerland). (Risk considerations may factor, however, in setting dividend policy or determining SOEs' strategy and objectives.)

Figure 3.1. **Approaches to determining the state's risk tolerance level**

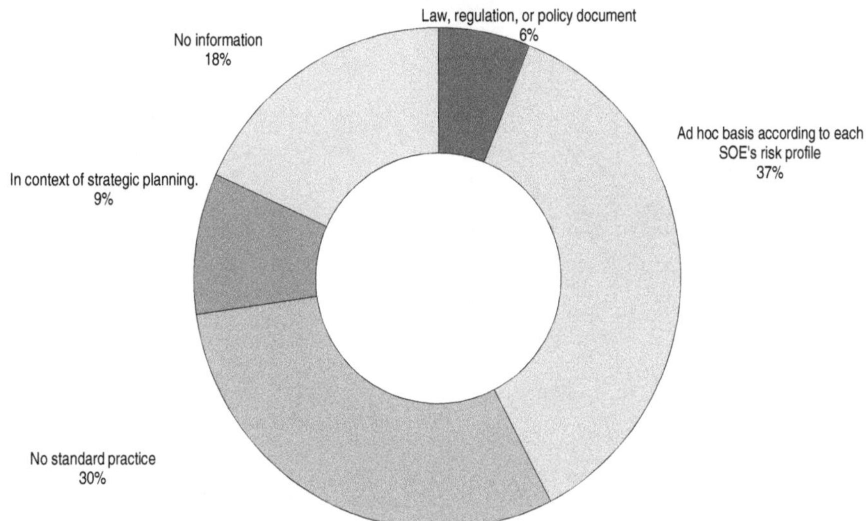

Source: Responses to the Working Party risk management questionnaire as of July 2016

Figure 3.2. **Avenues for communicating the state's risk tolerance level**

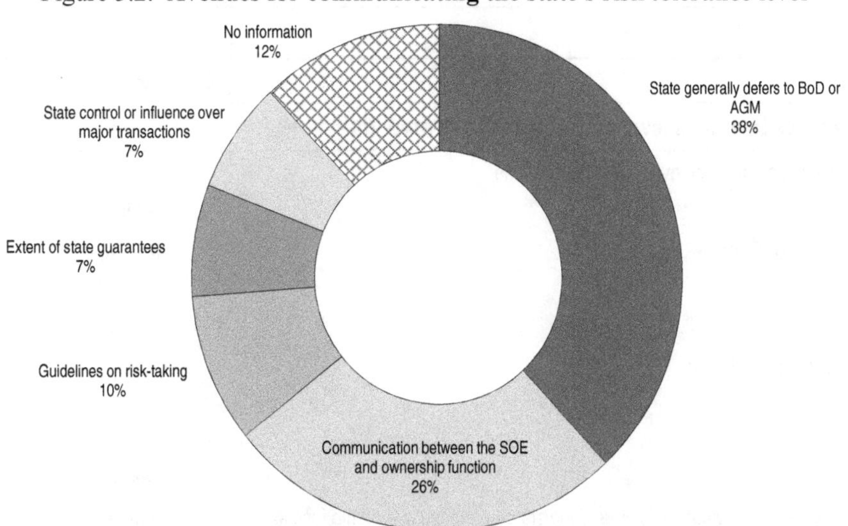

Source: Responses to the Working Party risk management questionnaire as of July 2016. Governments may apply more than one avenue for communicating their risk tolerance level.

Table 3.1. **Determining and communicating the state's risk tolerance level (Q10-11; see Annex A)**

	Countries
The State's risk tolerance level is determined:	
1. Via sector-wide and explicit law, regulation, decision or policy document	– **Philippines** – **Poland** – **Turkey**
2. On an *ad hoc* or as-needed basis, and according to each SOE's risk profile	– **Austria** – **Czech Republic** – **Denmark** – **Finland** – **Iceland** – **Ireland** – **Netherlands** – **Norway** – **Sweden** – **Switzerland** – **United Kingdom**
3. There is no standard practice	– **Brazil** – **Germany** – **Israel** – **Latvia** – **Mexico** – **New Zealand** – **Portugal** – **Slovenia** – **Spain**
4. In the broader context of overall strategic planning.	– **Chile** – **Lithuania**

	Countries
The State's risk tolerance level may be communicated via[1]:	
1. State control or influence over major transactions	– **Argentina** – **Latvia[2]**
2. Extent of state guarantees	– **Argentina** – **Czech Republic** – **Iceland**
3. Guidelines on risk-taking	– **China** – **Israel** – **Mexico** – **Poland**
4. Communication between the SOE and the state enterprise ownership function	– **Belgium** – **China** – **Chile**

	Countries
The State's risk tolerance level may be communicated via[1]:	
	– **Denmark** – **Finland** – **Ireland** – **Lithuania** – **New Zealand** – **Netherlands** – **Portugal** – **Slovenia** – **Turkey**
5. The State defers to the board of directors or AGM to set the risk appetite, within the parameters of the risk governance framework	– **Austria** – **Belgium** – **China** – **Finland** – **France** – **Germany** – **Ireland** – **Kazakhstan** – **Latvia** – **Netherlands** – **Norway** – **Philippines** – **Sweden** – **Switzerland** – **Turkey** – **United Kingdom**

1. Some governments may apply more than one channel for communicating risk tolerance levels to SOEs.
2. The state enterprise ownership function in Latvia is exercised by line ministries and public institutions. Practices vary across agencies, but some require shareholder approval for major transactions, such as the Ministry of Health, which must approve public procurement purchases over EUR140 000.

Source: Responses to the Working Party risk management questionnaire as of July 2016.

Table 3.2. **Consideration of risk tolerance levels in setting rates of return and leverage ratios (Q12; see Annex A)**

Country	Risk tolerance level is considered by the State when setting SOE rates of return (RoR)		Risk tolerance level is considered by the State when setting SOE leverage ratios	
	Yes	*No*	*Yes*	*No*
Argentina		✓ Set by AGM		✓
Austria		✓		✓
Belgium		✓		✓
Brazil		✓		✓
Chile	✓		✓	
China	✓		✓	
Czech Rep.		✓ Set by board		
Denmark	✓			
Finland		✓ Risk considered for dividend policy		✓
France				
Germany		✓		✓
Greece				
Iceland		✓[1]		✓
Ireland	✓		✓	
Israel		✓ Risk considered for budget-planning		✓
Italy				
Japan				
Kazakhstan		✓		✓
Latvia	✓			✓
Lithuania	✓		✓	
Mexico		✓		✓
Netherlands	✓		✓	
New Zealand		✓ Set by board		✓ Set by board
Norway	✓			
Philippines	✓		✓	
Poland		✓ Risk considered for dividend policy and setting strategic goals		

Country	Risk tolerance level is considered by the State when setting SOE rates of return (RoR)		Risk tolerance level is considered by the State when setting SOE leverage ratios	
	Yes	*No*	*Yes*	*No*
Portugal				
Slovenia	✓		✓	
Spain				
Sweden		✓ Set by AGM		✓ Set by AGM
Switzerland		✓	✓	
Turkey		✓		✓
United Kingdom				

1. Iceland authorities report that financial policy guidelines were under consideration as of October 2016 that could address risk considerations vis-à-vis SOE rates of return.

Source: Responses to the Working Party risk management questionnaire as of July 2016.

Nominations to, and remuneration of, SOE boards

The SOE Guidelines recommend that the agencies exercising the state ownership rights ensure that SOEs have efficient and well-functioning professional boards, with the required mix of competencies to fulfil their responsibilities.[4] When it comes to expertise in risk governance, only four countries report that risk-management skills are explicitly considered in director nominations (China, Ireland, Norway and the United Kingdom), while risk is explicitly considered when assessing director independence in five countries (Czech Republic, Denmark and Finland, Norway, and the United Kingdom). The board's ability to manage risk is considered in setting director remuneration in Brazil, the Czech Republic, Norway, and Switzerland. In addition, New Zealand was at the time of writing undertaking a review of its director remuneration methodology, with a view to developing a new framework that would more comprehensively address directors' management of three types of risk: revenue capital risk, liability risk, and public perception profile risk. (See Table 3.4, at the end of the next section, for a cross-country comparison of governments' approaches to nominations to, and remuneration of, SOE boards.)

In practice, a number of countries reported that the risk expertise of a nominee to the board or the risk expertise of the board as a whole is often considered when filling director vacancies (Denmark, Finland, France, Germany, Israel, Kazakhstan, Sweden, and Switzerland).[5]

State supervision of SOE risk management systems

Twenty-six of the 33 countries (79%) contributing to this stocktaking reported that they undertake some form of review of SOEs' internal risk management systems. Countries may employ more than one method for undertaking such reviews. The most common avenues for ownership entities' review of SOEs' risk management systems included: reviews undertaken by the ownership function (11 countries); via SOEs' activity reports (10 countries); via participation in or engagement with the board (6 countries); and/or via the AGM (7 countries) (see Figure 3.3). For example, in Brazil, the

Secretary of Coordination and Governance of State Enterprises (SEST) recently created a unit to evaluate SOEs in a broad sense, including financial results, public policies, governance practices, and also risk management. Brazil's CGU also developed a Guidebook of Compliance for State-Owned Companies to help SOEs address fraud- and corruption-related compliance risk, as well as a companion Evaluation of the Compliance of State-Owned Enterprises. (See Table 3.3, below, for a cross-country comparison of governments' approaches to ensuring SOE risk management.)

The role of state audit institutions

Twenty-two countries (67%) report that their state audit institutions perform audits of SOEs in their jurisdictions.[6] In 17 of these 20 countries, audits may include reviews of SOEs' risk management systems. In eight, audit institutions may also audit the state ownership function for their supervision of risk governance in the SOE sector. For example, in France, the Cour des Comptes may audit the state's ownership function, exercised by l'Agence des participations de l'État (APE), and the audit can be made public. In most cases, audits are undertaken systematically. Audits are more often both financial and performance-based (in 12 countries), but can also be strictly focused on financial results (in four countries) or on performance (in two countries). In cases where state audit institutions do not exercise direct oversight over SOEs, they may nevertheless become involved in some cases on an *ad hoc* or as-needed basis, for example, where SOEs receive subsidies from the state ("value for money" audits) and more generally where significant fiscal risks are perceived. (See Table 3.4 for highlights of national practices for state audits of SOEs and Table 3.5 for a cross-country comparison of state audit institutions' role in ensuring SOE risk governance.)

Figure 3.3 **Methods for undertaking state review of SOE risk management systems**

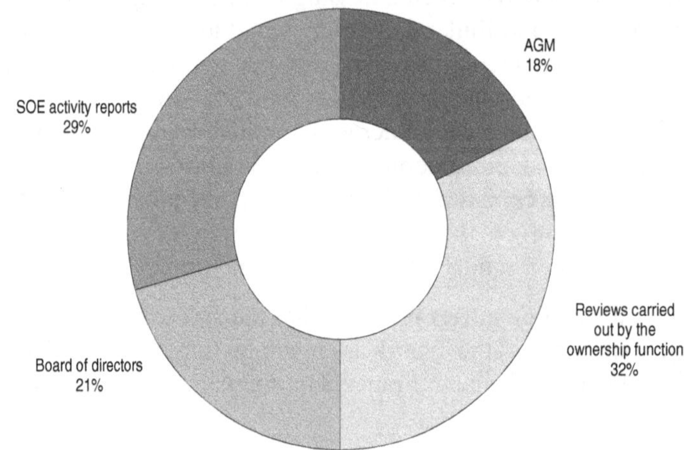

Source: Responses to the Working Party risk management questionnaire as of July 2016. Governments may apply more than one method for reviewing SOEs' risk management systems.

Table 3.3. **The role of the State in ensuring SOE risk management (Q13-15; see Annex A)**

Country	Ownership function reviews risk management systems	Board nominations by the ownership function:		Risk is considered in director remuneration
		Risk expertise of directors / the board are explicitly considered	*Risk is considered when assessing director independence*	
Argentina	●			
Austria	●			
Belgium	●			
Brazil	●			●
Chile				
China		o		
Czech Rep.	●		o	●
Denmark	●		o	
Finland	●		o	
France				
Germany				
Greece				
Iceland				
Ireland	●	o		
Israel	●			
Italy				
Japan	●			
Kazakhstan	●			
Latvia	●			
Lithuania	●			
Mexico	●			
Netherlands	●			
New Zealand	●			
Norway	●	o	o	●
Philippines	●			
Poland	●			
Portugal	●			
Slovenia	●			
Spain	●			
Sweden	●			
Switzerland	●			●
Turkey	●			
United Kingdom	●	o	o	

Source: Responses to the Working Party risk management questionnaire as of July 2016.

Table 3.4. **Highlights of national practices in 13 countries for state audits of SOEs**

Involvement	Category	Country	Description of audit practices
Most direct involvement of the state audit function	State audit function is regularly engaged with individual SOEs	Argentina	Argentina has two control agencies, established by Law No. 24.156. The first is the Comptroller General's Office, the Sindicatura General de la Nación (SIGEN). SIGEN attends (but does not vote) in board meetings, shareholders' meetings and meetings of the audit committee. SIGEN also coordinates SOEs' internal audit functions. The second is the General Audit Office (AGN) under the National Congress. The AGN's responsibilities include undertaking financial, accounting, and management audits of SOEs.
		Brazil	All SOEs are audited by two specialized public institutions: the CGU, and the Federal Court of Accounts. The CGU provides SOEs' internal audit functions with a risk matrix to guide audit planning (as required by the CGU). This audit planning is approved by the Board with a summary description of the risks attached to each audited item. The risk matrix evaluates the probability and impact of risks on firms' objectives.
		Iceland	The State Audit oversees the appointment of accountants for most SOEs and holds regular meetings with these accountants to discuss the enterprises' financial position. If the State Audit believes that risk is existent, then it is reported in the State Audit´s report on the State Account. The State Audit also issues various reports on risk management confronted by the State. In recent years, examples of such risks have increased.
↑	SOEs regularly audited by the state audit function	Denmark	The state audit agency audits SOEs fully owned by the state, or where the state has majority ownership. The audit is not only financial but also administrative, which means that the audit examines whether due financial considerations have been taken when administrating funds. The audits can include assessments of the risk management systems in the SOEs and potentially also assessments of the risk management conducted by the state with regard to its SOE portfolio.
		Latvia	The Supreme Audit Institution of the Republic of Latvia (State Audit Office, SAO) may perform compliance and performance audits of SOEs. The selection of audit topics and target SOEs is based upon an annual risk assessment by SAO auditors for each sector of the Latvian economy. During the pre-audit planning phase, the SAO first assesses SOEs' internal control systems, which includes an assessment of risk management policies and practices. The compliance and performance audits of SOEs undertaken by the SAO include an assessment of governance policies and practices of SOEs and of the state enterprise ownership function. Financial audits of SOEs' annual financial statements are performed by certified external auditors. The SAO relies on the external auditors' results when auditing the consolidated state budget. These audit reports are categorized and assessed as part of the State's long-term investments, since SOEs as legal entities are not included in the State's consolidated financial statement.
		Mexico	The Congress Federal Audit Office (Auditoría Superior de la Federación, ASF) is responsible for overseeing federal public resources invested in SOEs. The ASF reviews risk management through: (1) Performance audits (as per the Ley de Fiscalización y Rendición de Cuentas de la Federación, Law on Supervision and Accountability of the Federation), and (2) Oversight and review of the Federal Public Treasury Report (as per the Law on Supervision and Accountability of the Federation), which culminates with a Results Report (Informe de Resultados de la Revisión de la Cuenta Pública), which is presented to the Chamber of Deputies.
		Switzerland	According to the Federal Audit Act (art. 8), all SOEs are subject to financial oversight by the Federal Audit Office. (Listed SOEs are excepted, as they are subject to audit under the Stock Exchange Market Act). The Federal Audit Office audit jurisdiction also includes audit of SOE ownership entities, in order to assess their management systems for dealing with risks associated with state enterprise ownership.
		Turkey	SOEs under the portfolio of the Treasury are subject to annual compliance and performance audits by the Turkish Court of Accounts. The compliance and performance audit of SOEs aims to determine whether SOEs' activities are in line with laws, regulations, articles of association, etc., and whether the SOE's activity results are in line with the SOE's established objectives and performance indicators. The compliance and performance audit also includes an assessment of the SOE's efficiency and profitability.
Least direct involvement of the state audit function	SOEs audited as part of the state audit function's overall review of the public administration	Austria	The state audit agency ("Rechnungshof") conducts audits on the public federal administration and, generally speaking, majority owned SOEs, and it reports to the Austrian Parliament. The state audit agency will examine the management of SOEs with regard to completeness and accuracy of the figures provided, compliance with the applicable laws and, in particular, compliance of the management with the State's principles of frugality, expediency and profitability. There is no explicit provision in the Austrian State Audit Agency Act providing for the audit of a risk management system. Accordingly, the state audit agency will examine the risk management in the course of its examination of the SOEs´ management´s compliance with the applicable law. However, the state audit agency may conduct horizontal reviews on any relevant issue, including risk management.
		Finland	The state audit agency may every now and then survey and evaluate risks and risk management by SOEs, especially in cases of mismanagement.
		France	SOEs may be audited by the Cour des Comptes, which if necessary can prepare an audit report that can be made public. In the case of audits of SOEs and/or the ownership function, the Court may consider risk management.
		Japan	The "Board of Audit of Japan" audits the State accounts, as well as those of public organizations and other bodies as provided by the Board of Audit Act. The Board of Audit of Japan pays sufficient attention to the effectiveness of internal controls, including risk management by SOEs and by the State.
		Sweden	The Swedish National Audit Office (Sw. Riksrevisionen) regularly performs reviews with respect to the different governmental bodies' efficiency. [1]

1. See, for example, online here: http://www.riksrevisionen.se/en/Start/publications/Reports/EFF/2015/-The-Governments-management-of-risk-in-state-owned-enterprises-/

Source: Responses to the Working Party risk management questionnaire as of July 2016.

Table 3.5. **Role of state audit institutions in ensuring SOE risk governance (Q16; see Annex A)**

Country	State audit conducts audits of SOEs	Audits may review SOE risk systems	Audit focus (P/F/B)[1]	Audit frequency	Ownership entity may also be audited for supervision of SOE risk governance
Argentina	●		B	Systematically	
Austria	●	●	F		
Belgium	●	●	B	Systematically	
Brazil	●		B	Systematically	
Chile					
China					
Czech Rep.					
Denmark	●	●	B		●
Finland	●	●		As needed	
France	●	●	B	As needed	●
Germany					
Greece					
Iceland	●		F	Systematically	
Ireland					
Israel					
Italy					
Japan	●	●	B	As needed	●
Kazakhstan	●		B		
Latvia	●	●	P	Systematically	●
Lithuania	●	●		Systematically	
Mexico	●	●	P	Systematically	
New Zealand	●	●	F	Systematically	
Netherlands					●
Norway	●	●	B	As needed	●
Philippines	●	●	F	Systematically	
Poland	●	●	B	As needed	●
Portugal	●		B		
Slovenia					
Spain	●	●			
Sweden	●				
Switzerland	●	●	B	Systematically	●
Turkey	●	●	B	Systematically	
United Kingdom		●			

1. P = performance audit; F = financial audit; B = both performance and financial.

Source: Responses to the Working Party risk management questionnaire as of July 2016.

Notes

1. This is again consistent with the Corporate Governance Committee's 2014 review of SOE risk management practices, which included a similar list of mechanisms governments employ to determine and communicate the State's risk tolerance level. OECD (2014a) p. 22.
2. Exchange rate as of October 2015, 1 DKK = 0.13 EUR
3. The Chilean authorities further explain that, since 2001, Chile has conducted its fiscal policy based on fiscal rule. According to this rule, expenditures are defined year-by-year, so as to reach a certain target for the structural balance of the government. The structural balance is computed by adjusting actual public revenues by the cyclical position of the economy and by deviations of current copper prices from its long-term values, defined by a committee of experts. Thus, by using this rule, the government saves copper windfalls when the copper price is high, and is able to finance its deficits when the copper price is low, without compromising medium-term solvency.
4. See Chapter II.F.2 of the SOE Guidelines and annotations (OECD, 2015).
5. The 2014 Corporate Governance Committee review of SOE risk management noted that some respondents agreed on the position that the variable element of managerial remuneration in SOEs is so relatively limited that it does not encourage managers to take excessive risk. (OECD 2014a, p. 22) Countries contributing to this report did not make exactly the same statement, but some (such as Germany) noted that SOEs' budgets are set to avoid excessive risk-taking.
6. The United Kingdom is not included in the list of countries whose state audit institutions regularly audit SOEs. However, while the National Audit Office has no specific role regarding risk management by SOEs, its remit covers SOEs and it can seek to review/report on any or all procedures conducted by SOEs that might lead to financial risk.

References

OECD (2015), OECD Guidelines on Corporate Governance of State-Owned Enterprises, 2015 Edition, OECD Publishing, Paris. *http://dx.doi.org/10.1787/9789264244160-en.*

OECD (2014a), Risk Management and Corporate Governance, OECD Publishing, Paris. *http://dx.doi.org/10.1787/9789264208636-en.*

OECD (2014b), The Size and Sectoral Distribution of SOEs in OECD and Partner Countries, OECD Publishing, Paris. *http://dx.doi.org/10.1787/9789264215610-en org/10.1787/9789264208636-en.*

Annex A

Working Party on State Ownership and Privatisation Practices: Questionnaire on risk management by state-owned enterprises and their ownership

Questions

I. The legal and regulatory framework applicable to SOE risk governance

1. Please briefly outline the various legal forms under which SOEs may be incorporated in your jurisdiction.

2. Which laws, regulations, and/or codes address risk management by SOEs engaged in economic activities? Do the rules for SOEs differ from private companies in like circumstances? Also, if the rules differ according to legal forms of the SOE, please provide details.

3. Do these requirements apply to risk management in the general sense, or are they limited to the management of "material risk" (or some similar definition)? Please provide details, including the definition of materiality, if such a definition exists in your jurisdiction and applies in this context.

II. Risk management in practice at the level of the SOE

4. Please describe the requirements to which SOE boards of directors (if necessary broken down by the legal forms of SOEs) are subject in terms of the "duty of care". Is this duty specified vis-a-vis the owners, the company, or both?

5. Are SOE boards in your jurisdiction required to establish, or oversee the establishment of, internal risk management systems? If so, please provide an explanation of the scope of risks addressed by such systems[1]. Please also specify whether these requirements differ from those assigned to privately owned companies. If there are no formal requirements, have SOEs (or some SOEs) nevertheless in practice implemented such practices?

6. Are SOEs required to establish specific board committees charged with overseeing risk management? If so, please provide details, including whether this requirement also applies to privately owned companies.

7. Regarding material risk factors: (i) how are they identified by the board; (ii) how are they reported to the board; (iii) how frequently are such reports made to the board; and (iv) under what laws,

1. These can include financial risks (such as exchange rate risk) and non-financial risks, such as those identified in the Guidelines (i.e., public procurement risk [Guidelines III.G], compliance risk [Guidelines V.C], risk related to fulfilling responsible business conduct obligations [Guidelines V.D], conflict of interest risk [Guidelines V.E], risk associated with related party transactions [Guidelines VI.A.8]).

regulations or standards are such reports made? Where applicable, please specify where requirements for SOEs differ from those applicable to privately owned companies.

8. Are SOEs required to, or do they in practice, employ risk officers or other specialised staff dealing with risk management? If so, please provide an explanation of the scope of risks assessed by those executing the risk management function, as well as an explanation of their reporting lines to executive management and/or the board.

9. Please provide a practical example (or examples) of the internal risk management systems exercised by SOEs' executive management. Are the internal risk management systems assessed by an external auditor? By the SOEs' internal audit function?

III. Risk management in practice at the level of the State

10. How does the state ownership entity determine its risk tolerance level as regards its ownership stake in an SOE and/or for its stake in the authority's overall ownership portfolio?

11. How is risk tolerance communicated to individual SOEs? How does this differ in situations where the State has full ownership and where the State is not the sole owner (and hence not in a position to formally "mandate" the fulfilment of specific objectives)?

12. To what extent is the state ownership entity's risk tolerance level considered when setting target rates of return on SOEs' economic activities? Does the ownership entity set maximum leverage ratios for all or certain SOEs?

13. Does the state ownership entity review SOEs' internal risk management systems? If so, how (i.e., through regular reporting requirements, regular discussions with the board and/or management, or on an ad hoc or exceptional basis)?

14. Regarding the state ownership entity's role in nominating directors to the board, what steps are taken to ensure that the board: (a) has sufficient expertise to understand the risks incurred by the SOE, and (b) is sufficiently independent in order to adequately assess and address these risks?

15. Does the remuneration policy for SOE boards in your jurisdiction specifically address risk-taking by members of the board for the long- and medium-term interest of the SOE and its shareholders? If so, please provide details.

16. What is the role of the state audit agency with regard to risk management by SOEs and by the state with regards to its SOE portfolio?

ORGANISATION FOR ECONOMIC CO-OPERATION AND DEVELOPMENT

The OECD is a unique forum where governments work together to address the economic, social and environmental challenges of globalisation. The OECD is also at the forefront of efforts to understand and to help governments respond to new developments and concerns, such as corporate governance, the information economy and the challenges of an ageing population. The Organisation provides a setting where governments can compare policy experiences, seek answers to common problems, identify good practice and work to co-ordinate domestic and international policies.

The OECD member countries are: Australia, Austria, Belgium, Canada, Chile, the Czech Republic, Denmark, Estonia, Finland, France, Germany, Greece, Hungary, Iceland, Ireland, Israel, Italy, Japan, Korea, Latvia, Luxembourg, Mexico, the Netherlands, New Zealand, Norway, Poland, Portugal, the Slovak Republic, Slovenia, Spain, Sweden, Switzerland, Turkey, the United Kingdom and the United States. The European Union takes part in the work of the OECD.

OECD Publishing disseminates widely the results of the Organisation's statistics gathering and research on economic, social and environmental issues, as well as the conventions, guidelines and standards agreed by its members.

OECD PUBLISHING, 2, rue André-Pascal, 75775 PARIS CEDEX 16
(26 2016 03 1 P) ISBN 978-92-64-26221-8 – 2016

11.621 845149LV00010B/1846 [430086722]

www.ingramcontent.com/pod-product-compliance
Lightning Source LLC
LaVergne TN